TALES
OF A
TEXAS BOY

Marva Dasef

ISBN 978-1-4382-3545-5
LARGE PRINT EDITION

Copyrights

Rattlesnakes and Jackrabbits, first published in StoryStation, 2005.

The Corn Patch Incident, first published in Writers Post Journal, 2006.

The Cattle Drive, first published in Writers Post Journal, 2006.

One Fine Dog, first published in Writers Post Journal, 2006.

Mr. Young's Arkansas Cedar Float, first published in Writers Post Journal, 2006.

The Bone Hunters, first published in Long Story Short, 2006.

The Thief, first published in Antithesis Common, 2006.

Copyright © Marva Dasef

Texas Boy Publications

LARGE PRINT EDITION

ISBN 978-1-4382-3545-5

Printed and bound in the United States of America.

TALES OF A TEXAS BOY

Acknowledgments

FIRST AND FOREMOST, I'd like to thank my father for mustering up quite a few stories from his childhood. No mean feat for an octogenarian. I also need to thank him for overlooking the times I strayed from the absolute truth for literary license. For the most part, however, these stories have a seed, if not a full-grown fruit, of truth to them.

I must also thank all of my friends who read every story and commented helpfully on them as I wrote them. These people include Jenny Loftus, Eileen McBride, Diane Swint, Will Riley, and Bryan Catherman. I also received excellent critiques from a few writing groups. To these many writers and readers, I owe grateful recognition.

I wish to acknowledge with deep thanks The Handbook of Texas Online. This internet site proved a treasure trove of information on Texas. If you need to know anything about Texas, you can visit them here:

www.tsha.utexas.edu/handbook/online/index.html

Another valuable resource was the Portal to Texas History website. You can visit them here:

texashistory.unt.edu/searchform.tkl

Last and not least, I thank my dear husband Jack for reading every word and encouraging me to continue to work on these stories.

Foreword

WEST TEXAS IN the Depression era felt the sting of poverty covering the country. However, the Texans were to some extent spared the deep poverty more prevalent in the dustbowl just north of the Texas border.

The fact they could still produce food insulated farmers and ranchers, although much of the rest of society was left in poverty. Still, even these people were not entirely untouched. Times were tough, but people didn't complain, they just got along as best they could.

The stories included in this book take a look at the life of one boy and his family during that time.

§ § §

"We saw that big sign there and it said 'Free College'. I'd never heard of any such thing, so Red and me, we thought maybe we'd try it out. But, we didn't after all, 'cause we saw we could pick tomatoes. We went down there and signed up for a while. We went to the World's Fair, you know, in San Francisco. Later, me and Red enlisted in the army."

Animated now, my father, who isn't much of a conversationalist, was telling me about things he did in 1939. He and his buddy, Red, were on a road trip in a new 1940 Ford. They'd just graduated from high school and wanted to examine the world a bit beyond the tiny world of Salem High

School. He'd told me plenty of stories and I hurried up and wrote them down. Why hadn't I started this long ago?

The stories flowed, backtracked, started up again somewhere else. Sometimes, he was back in high school on the football team, sometimes in grade school, then forward again, bouncing wherever his eighty-four year old mind led him. His high school yearbook showed his picture with the words 'Ed the Cad'. Quite a heartbreaker back then, he was. The cool dude, sports jock, class president, too. Who was this guy?

As a kid growing up in West Texas, he'd gone on a cattle drive, collected bones to sell, encountered skunks in cornfields, went fishing with special Arkansas cedar floats. Good stories. Real life stories.

Later, he was Ed the logger, going after cheating log scalers with a double-bitted axe, leaving partners at the top of the pass in a blizzard. He made the big deals and we got rich...temporarily. Then, it all slid out of control and we were back on the road again.

When I was ten years old, he worked a deal clearing a man's land. A week's work to give his daughter a horse. And, what a horse! Old Ranger was a handful, but my ten-year-old self could handle the sixteen-hand saddlebred...mostly. One day, Ranger didn't want to be ridden, so he hauled off and kicked me twenty feet across the field. I went crying to my daddy. He caught Ranger, all right, and rode him hard until Ranger stood with sides heaving, all the fight gone. Until then,

I never knew my father could even ride, much less ride like a cowboy.

My father passed away in 2011, but his almost true tall tales continue on in this book.

Why did it take me until he is near his end to ask him? Why did it take me so long to write the stories he had to tell? These are his stories. I call them the "Little Eddie in Texas" stories and warn people that I'd come up with another one from the kid who lived in a different time and with a different life than any of us will ever know.

Welcome to Little Eddie's world. I hope you enjoy the ride.

Dad Boles and Sophie

During the 1930's in the rural region of West Texas, working was just about all people had time to do. However, even without television or access to movie houses, there was still some entertainment for the masses. The county fair became a yearly highlight for the farm families. Sometimes, the entertainment wasn't inside the gate to the fair, but outside where a few folks who were just a bit different set up their own type of show.

IT WAS SUMMER again and the carnival would be here in a week. That's about the most exciting event of the year, except maybe the roundup and branding. I surely was looking forward to the cotton candy and riding the Ferris wheel. Beins I'm a kid, a carnival was pretty interesting, but I looked forward to it most 'cause that's when Dad Boles came to town.

My Pa met up with Dad Boles during the war where they'd been in France with the cavalry. My Pa was the horse doctor and Dad Boles was the horseshoer, though he'd been a lot of different things in his life. They'd hit it off and Dad Boles took to coming to

Hereford to spend time with Pa and to bring his bear to the carnival.

I didn't mention he owned a bear? Oh, he surely did! He'd raised Sophie from a cub. Truth be known I think he'd killed her ma, so he wasn't exactly being overly nice by taking in a little bear cub. He also kept a pet bobcat named Bob.

When they all drove up to the farm in his big Studebaker, they surely were a sight. Sophie sat up in the back seat just like she was a person. Bob rode in a cage as he wasn't as easy-goin' as Sophie.

The rest of the Studebaker was loaded full of bobcat skins, which Dad Boles sold at the carnival. He'd set himself a place just outside the carnival entrance, so everybody had to walk by him on the way in. He laid the skins out around a heavy pole he'd pounded into the ground. He tied Sophie's leash to the pole. She leaned up against it and sat up on her haunches. Her big head waved back and forth as she snuffed at the smell of the food sold by the carnies. Ever once in awhile, Dad Boles would toss her sumpin to eat. She seemed to be just fine with watchin' the people go by.

After I'd spent the dollar Pa gave me at the carnival, which took me only an hour, I'd go outside the gate and spend my time with Dad Boles. That was right near as entertaining as the two-headed calf in the tent show.

A lot of folks stopped to look at the skins, too. Dad Boles didn't make any pitch to 'em. They'd ask how much, and he said fifty cents and that was that. No wheelin' or dealin'. Most who wanted a skin thought it was a good price anyways.

Now, it was an entirely different business when it came to Sophie. Every year it was the same. Farmers brought their dogs to the carnival, just 'cause Sophie was there. They'd bet on whether their dogs could take Sophie or not. Now, you'd think with Sophie tied up and all, the dogs would have a good shot at her. But that'd be cruel and Dad Boles loved Sophie and wouldn't see her come to any harm. Nor, did he want the dogs hurt. The bet was whether the dog could get to the bear and, if'n it did, it'd be pulled back real quick.

Lots of folks brought their dogs to test Sophie, but also just to come watch the game. It surely was an interesting crowd of people. The farmers were there in the coveralls, the cowboys wearing their best hats. Even some town folk would stop by to take a look. I recall Mrs. Oakes come round. I tried not to laugh when I saw her 'cause she liked to wear really big hats, all covered with fruit and flowers. It was particularly amusing as she also carried around her own little dog, which she named Mimi 'cause it was a French dog. It weren't any bigger than a squirrel so she tucked it up under her arm like a package.

Those dogs were gettin' bigger and meaner every year and I began to worry whether Sophie'd still be able to stop 'em. The dog owners didn't seem to care much whether their dogs or Sophie'd get hurt. That did bother me some as I naturally loved all animals. Beasts of the field, Pa called 'em. I didn't quite understand that 'cause I didn't see neither bear nor dog as being a field critter.

I'd heard Dad Boles tell Pa how he'd trained Sophie to be gentle with the dogs. He'd also cut her claws back to nubs before the carnival. So, he'd made sure Sophie wouldn't kill the dogs. He made sure the dogs wouldn't harm Sophie by packin' a Colt Peacemaker at his belt. He kept it in the holster, but I'd seen him whip it out as fast as any gunslinger. I figured if one of the dogs got close to Sophie, he'd shoot it. Never had to, at least as I observed.

One year, a rancher brought along a special dog with the direct idea of beating Sophie. It were a big brute. Musta weighed a hundred-fifty at least. Pa told me he was a mastiff. He didn't seem to be a mean dog as he was wagging his tail and generally seemed friendly. Still, that changed when he caught Sophie's scent. Later, I found out the man trained the dog to fight using bearskins. He'd wrap the skin around his arm and hit the dog with a stick, so's the dog connected the bear smell with the beating.

The dog started pulling at his leash and growling. He didn't pay no attention to anything else but that bear. The man could hardly hold the dog back whilst they laid the bet.

The usual bet was fifty cents or so, and Dad Boles made quite a bit just from that. The man musta been confident his dog could take Sophie 'cause he slapped down a hundred-dollar bill on the pile of bobcat skins.

Dad Boles looked at the dog and looked at the hundred, considering. That was a lot of money, but he wasn't too eager to shoot the dog as he thought he might have to do.

He says, "All right, it's a bet," and pulled out his money bag and threw it down with the hundred. "There's plenty enough there to cover."

The man grinned an evil grin. He surely did think his dog could get to Sophie, and he didn't seem to realize Dad Boles would shoot the dog if'n he did get close to the bear.

The rancher let go of the leash and the dog sprung forward so fast it'd knock your hat right off. He was snarling so mean at the same time, so's your skin would crawl. I held my breath, just like everybody else standin' there.

Sophie looked at the dog heading her way, but only seemed mildly interested. The dog got to about three feet from her throat and she slapped her big paw out like it was on a spring. She hit the dog right in his chops and he went a'flying.

The dog landed with a thud and he lay there stunned for a few seconds. Everybody held still waitin' to see if'n Sophie'd finally killed a dog.

All a sudden, the dog jumped up on all fours and proceeded to run just as fast as his legs would carry him, yiping for all he was worth the whole time.

Dad Boles grinned at the man, whose mouth was hanging open. Dad scooped up the hundred along with his moneybag and put both away in his coat.

"Better go find yer dog," he said as he threw a hot dog to Sophie. She snapped it up in midair, looking a mite proud of herself.

Whilst everybody was distracted lookin' to see if the big dog was hurt or not, Mrs. Oakes' little dog Mimi jumped down out of her arms and tore on up to Sophie barkin' for all she was worth. Everybody gasped and held their breath, thinkin' Sophie would just take one bite and that little dog wouldn't be no more. By then, Mimi'd grabbed hold of Sophie's paw and was worrying it sumpin fierce. Sophie just looks down all calm. Then gentle as can be, she gave the little dog a light tap with one toe of one paw. Mrs. Oakes ran right up to Sophie and grabbed up Mimi. She rushed away crying "oh, my poor little baby!"

Dad Boles looked relieved that Sophie showed such good sense. He turned to the crowd and said, "good thing nobody bet on that dog."

Rattlesnakes and Jackrabbits

Domestic livestock weren't the only animals that the farmers and ranchers had to deal with. The wildlife of the region didn't hide out in the bushes all the time. Sometimes they were pretty much in your face. Rattlesnakes came to the farms to catch the rats and mice that populated granaries. Rabbits also took a liking to the easy pickings. Both animals, rattlesnakes and jackrabbits, ended up being a nuisance that the local farmers and ranchers had to control.

TEXANS LIKE TO brag everything is bigger in Texas. That might be a little exaggeration, but with two things I think it's pretty much the truth. In Texas, rattlesnakes and jackrabbits come in three sizes: big, bigger, and biggest. I'm also of a mind there are more of each of these critters per square mile than fleas on a stray dog.

You couldn't walk across the farmyard without spottin' at least one rattler. Pa was kept plenty busy just keepin' the rattlers away from the house. The snakes liked to stay around the granary where they'd find plenty of rats to eat. While we appreciated their service, getting rid of the rats, it was dangerous havin' them around the farmyard. I was old enough to watch out for the snakes, but the little kids wouldn't be fast enough to avoid them. Pa had no choice but to kill the snakes when we'd find one.

Pa told me once a hair rope would keep out a rattler, so I wondered why we didn't just put a real long rope 'round the yard. Pa said it only works when you're camping out. That puzzled me some. I asked him why it worked only then and he tol' me the rope circle had to be small, just enough to surround you when you're sleepin'. I could see how that might be true, so I asked him why it worked at all. He said, "Eddie, it's because the rattlers are superstitious."

We didn't see the jackrabbits as often, but we knew when they'd come in the middle of the night 'cause we'd see the holes they'd gnaw in the granary walls. The better the crop, the more jackrabbits there'd be. I guessed the one would beget t'other. Around these parts, we called them deer rabbits as they appeared to be as big as deer. Of course, that was also just a joke, but if you see a jackrabbit's ears sticking up behind a mesquite bush, you'd swear it was bigger'n the seven or eight pounds they'd usually weigh.

Because the local farmers and ranchers saw 'em both as a big problem, on occasion they'd get together and go hunting. This mostly happened in the spring or fall when the rattlers were birthing. The reason was if they found a rattler's den, they could kill upwards of a hundred babies at one time. In the meantime, the men could also be looking for jackrabbits.

Up to fifteen, twenty men would fire up their trucks and

head out with their .22s and a bunch of boxes to collect up the jackrabbits. The jackrabbits were tough, but could still make a passable stew, so no sense in letting 'em go to waste.

A big part of this expedition included moonshine. The hunters would head out in the early afternoon and start drinking right off. By dusk, most of 'em couldn't hit much of anything, but was havin' a lotta fun anyways. The hardest part of the trip was avoidin' being shot by somebody else. Mostly, though, these men knew what they was doing even when they could hardly see straight. I was glad Pa wasn't a drinker as I'd see how stupid the men would act. I guess that would be one more reason why I respected my Pa.

When I turned twelve, Pa let me go along on a hunt. Course, I didn't drink no moonshine, but I already had my own .22 rifle and was getting to be a fair shot. My Pa doesn't kill animals for sport and neither do I, but we had a farm to run and both the rattlers and the jackrabbits were causin' enough problems that we had to do it.

I'll admit, I did enjoy goin' out with the men. It was fun to be bouncing around in the back of Pa's Model A truck scanning the prairie for either of the offending beasts. If'n anybody spotted sumpin, we'd stop and get out of the cars and the trucks and start hunting on foot. We'd all go in different directions so as to cover the most ground.

We'd found a den of rattlesnake babies. There must of been a hundred or more, none of 'em over six inches long. They were small, but plenty feisty as they coiled up and shook their little one-button rattles just like the big ones. I turned aside as I didn't want to watch. It's one thing shootin' at sumpin from afar, but the men were stomping on the little snakes to kill 'em. It turned my stomach, so I went off in another direction.

I was going along pretty slow, so I wouldn't step in a snake hole when I heard the squeal of a rabbit in pain. A lot of folks don't realize rabbits make a sound like that. It'd send shivers up your spine. I went quick toward the sound and found a bullsnake at least six-foot long if he were an inch. He was all coiled around a baby cottontail and his mouth was gaped open holdin' onto the rabbit. The poor little rabbit was half swallowed, but the snake made the mistake of tryin' ta swallow it from the rear instead of the head. The cottontail was strugglin' and screamin' so much the snake looked downright annoyed.

Now, we don't hunt bullsnakes, as they're the natural enemy of rattlesnakes. And, we don't hunt cottontails, as they weren't big enough to do much harm. We pretty much left them both alone. The sound of the little rabbit's screaming just 'bout broke my heart. I run up to them and stepped down on the snake's neck just back of the lump that was the rabbit's rear end. That stopped the swallowing, but now I wasn't sure what to do. I laid down my .22, grabbed the cottontail by the ears and commenced pullin'. A bullsnake's teeth point backwards, so the rabbit was pretty much stuck in the snake's mouth.

I was tuggin' and the rabbit's cryin' and the snake's

whippin' round trying to get my foot off'n his neck. No progress was being made by any of the three of us.

My Pa heard the rabbit, too, and he came running over and saw the fix I'd got myself into. He started to laugh some, but when he looked me in the eyes, he stopped right quick. He started pryin' the snake's mouth open trying to unhook the teeth from the rabbit. I let up pullin' to allow Pa to work the rabbit loose.

Soon enough, we'd got the rabbit out of the snake's mouth and Pa set the little guy down easy. I reached down and grabbed the bullsnake by the neck where I'd been standing and flung him as far as I could. He hit the ground slithering and was gone in a second. Pa and me took a look at the cottontail, which looked somewhat bedraggled. He was laying there pantin' and started tryin' to pull hisself with his front legs. It looked like he'd got a broke back and I thought we'd have to put him out of his misery.

Pa picked up his .22 and started to draw a bead on the cottontail's head when it looked up at him with those big ol' eyes. He stayed his hand. "Maybe he's just stunned," he said.

While we stood there watchin' the rabbit, a couple of the men came up to see what we'd found. Pa told them about the bullsnake and they thought it a pretty good joke I'd try to save a rabbit from a snake.

After a bit, the rabbit started to move his hind legs a little. He hunched them up under him and inched his way into the underbrush.

We went back to the truck and Pa decided we'd had enough hunting. Neither one of us had the heart to kill anything, at least not that day. I hoped the cottontail recovered and went about his business. I also hoped the bullsnake went off an found himself a meal, but I was glad it wasn't my cottontail. Life is hard on the prairie, but there ain't no sense in relishing the death of any animal, not even a rattlesnake or a jackrabbit.

The Auction

Mules and jackasses have a special place on the farm. They're strong and tough, so farms back in the early part of the twentieth century couldn't operate without them. Fortunately, or sometimes unfortunately, they were also very smart and had a mind of their own.

PA HOLLERED AT me. "Eddie, you get outta bed and get dressed."

I looked out the window and saw it was still dark, so I knew sumpin must be up. I jumped up and pulled on my pants and boots as fast as I could. I grabbed up a shirt and headed down the ladder from the loft where I sleep.

When I get to the kitchen, I saw Ma was already cooking up some ham n' eggs. My stomach started growling at the smell, so I finished buttoning my shirt and tucked it in like Ma likes. Sumpin was definitely going on since we usually do chores before we get breakfast.

"I thought you was going to sleep all day, Eddie," Pa says when he sees me plop down in my chair.

"Pa, it's still dark out," I said and Pa gave me the look what told me I was statin' the obvious. I looked through the doorway at the chime clock in the sitting room and saw it was only four in the morning. We usually get to sleep 'til five, so I was starting to get real curious.

"We're going up to Amarillo to an auction. They brought in some mules from Georgia and I thought to take a look."

I knew about the auction, but I didn't know we was going to it. After all, we raised mules, so I wondered why we'd buy some more.

"Yessir. Those Georgia mules are special I hear." If Pa wanted to buy mules from Georgia, that was his business. But I weren't going to argue, as a trip to Amarillo didn't happened every day.

"They also brought in a couple of jacks if you was wondering why I'd want to look at mules," Pa said when he read my thoughts from my expression. I weren't very good at hiding things from Pa. Not that I was trying to hide nothing. I just didn't want to question his good sense, especially at four in the morning.

We finished up eating breakfast and got ready to hit the road to Amarillo. Ma gave us a sack with some biscuits and leftover ham, so we'd have something to eat along the way. I helped Pa push the truck out of the barn and he cranked it while I worked the throttle. Soon enough, we were driving north to the big city.

We pulled the truck into the fairgrounds where the auction was going on. There were trucks and cars all over the place. I hadn't seen so many folks together in one place since the last county fair. Most everybody was milling around the holdin' pens looking over the stock. There weren't just mules, but also horses, cows, and pigs. Each of the types had a different time to be auctioned. It meant folks who were interested in any animal auctioned later had to sit through stock they didn't care about. Everybody had to come first thing, since it wasn't known 'til then when any one auction was going to start.

But, there was plenty to do if'n you had to wait. It was interesting just looking over the stock and seeing what was up for sale. Some traveling salesmen set up booths where they'd pitch their wares. They was right entertaining just to watch. Those fellas sure could talk! They was selling everything you could think of. One fella was selling a potion to cure the bellyache and baldness all at the same time. I couldn't rightly figure how it could work. Still, he swore it come from a old Indian who never had a bellyache and sure weren't bald, so it must work. I ain't never seen a bald Indian, so I had to believe him.

There weren't no beef cattle for sale, as they are sold in herds not one animal at a time. They did have milk cows, though. Pa and me was looking over a Holstein, just about the biggest cow I ever did see. The auctioneer went from pen to pen auctioning off the animals.

The crowd of buyers followed him around and bid on the ones they wanted. When they got to the Holstein, Pa and me were already in the pen inspecting the cow. The auctioneer come into the pen and pushed on the cow to move her aside. The cow stepped right on my foot. I didn't think it polite to yell out, so I just tried to shove on the cow to get her to step off.

"You move aside, boy," the auctioneer said.

"Yessir. I'm tryin' to," I answered.

Pa walked around from the other side of the cow and saw I'm stuck, so he gave the cow a big push so she'd step off'n my foot. I'm glad I wore my cowboy boots or she woulda broke my foot for sure. I decided I'd stay out of the pens from there on out.

The auctioneer bid up the cow and she went for the nice price of thirty-five dollars. The bunch of us moved on to the next pen. Pa and I watched as they sold off a heifer, then a nice-sized sow.

After a while, we reached the pens where they stabled the mules. I knew Pa wasn't interested in the mules as we breed them ourselves, so we just waited through the bidding until it got to something interesting.

We came to an empty pen and we all walked by. Then, another empty pen and we moved on past that one, too. Finally, we came to the end of the line of pens and lined up in front of the one holding an animal. There weren't a single horse, cow, mule, or pig within three pens of the one where we found ourselves at last.

I looked in and my jaw dropped like a rock. There stood the biggest, blackest, and meanest looking jackass I ever did see. Two men were holding lead ropes tied to his halter. His head was up and he was puffing his nostrils as he stood there stiff up against the back of the pen. The lead ropes were stretched to their fullest and the two men didn't look too happy to be in the pen with this critter.

He were at least eighteen hands, so he was near as tall as Pa. His head reared up another three feet. Maybe you'll think I'm exaggeratin', but I swear it's the truth. He was the biggest Mammoth Jack I ever did see.

The bunch of men standing outside the pen were mumbling to each other and looking at the auction book. Pa was holding a copy, so I asked for it and read about the farm he come from in Georgia and other such information.

The auctioneer started up, "What am I bid for this fine jack?"

"Ten," I heard from the other side of the crowd. All a sudden, the jackass reared up against the ropes and one of the men holding him got flung up on the fence. The other one dropped the rope and scrambled over the side of the pen.

The Jack threw his head down and went for the man who was on the ground. The beast's mouth was gaped open and he was clearly trying to do some serious damage. Men outside the pen jumped up and grabbed the hands of the man in the pen and jerked him right out. The Jack reared up and slammed his front hooves against the side of the gate.

Crack! The gate splintered and the Jack came tearing out. A brave man grabbed hold of the ropes but he just got hauled behind the jackass like he was no more'n a sheet flyin' in the wind. Another in the crowd with some presence of mind opened the gate across the alleyway and the Jack went into the next pen. A bunch of the fellas slammed the gate shut.

"Oh, c'mon folks, this Jack is only four years old. He's worth a lot more'n that. Who'll give me fifteen?"

Nobody said anything for a bit, then Pa held up his auction card and said "Fifteen."

The auctioneer pointed at Pa and grinned. I believe he thought the bidding was just getting started.

"Do I hear twenty? Twenty. Twenty. I've got fifteen. Who'll give me twenty?"

Nobody said a word.

"Gentlemen, I can't believe you won't bid on this fine animal. Just look at the hip on this outfit. He weighs in at over fifteen hundred pounds."

The auctioneer looked around at the silent crowd. He tried one more time.

"He'll be a fine stud. Your mules will be big, strong fellas. C'mon now, I've got fifteen. Give me seventeen, seventeen. Alright, give me sixteen."

It didn't do no good. The crowd figured any jackass that could break down a two by twelve board gate was more'n they wanted to deal with.

"Sold to the gentleman in the Stetson," the auctioneer finished. He knew when to give up and move on. Pa had just bought himself a new jackass.

The rest of the crowd moved on. Pa and me stood there and looked at the Jack. The big fella snorted a few times and stamped his hoof on the ground, but seemed to be over most of his mad.

Everything was finally quiet while me and Pa pondered what to do next. Then, I heard a snuffling sound, but it didn't come from the jackass. I looked over to the next pen and saw a boy sitting on the ground, hunched over. I could see he was crying and it made me wonder. Pa looked over, too.

"What's the matter, boy?"

The boy, who was not much older than me, looked up and wiped his nose on his sleeve.

"Nothin', sir," he answered in a quavery voice.

"Well, you must be sad about sumpin." Pa opened the gate to the pen the boy was in and patted him on the shoulder.

"Why not tell us about it? We'll try to help if we can."

"Well, sir, that jackass belonged to my daddy up 'til you bought him. Times are hard, so he was forced to sell. I've raised up Samson from a foal. I'm just gonna miss him sumpin fierce."

"We'll take good care of him. I promise," Pa said and took the boy by the shoulder. He stood him up and reached out his hand.

"You got my word, son. Can we shake on it?"

The boy reached out and shook Pa's hand.

"Alright. I guess that's fair. I'll miss ol' Samson, but you seem a nice man who'll take care of him right."

"I sure will, son. What's your name?"

"Robert Ray James, but folks call me jus' Bobby Ray."

Bobby Ray went into the pen with Samson. Pa got kind of tense as he'd seen how the jackass was. But, the boy walked right up to the Jack and threw his arms around the big neck. Samson put his nose down and nuzzled the boy's shoulder for a minute. I heard the boy whisper, but I couldn't make out what he said. I kind of thought he was saying goodbye.

Then, Bobby Ray picked up the lead ropes and handed them over to Pa.

"He'll be good for you now, sir. I tol' him to behave hisself." Bobby Ray walked away and didn't look back even when Samson threw his head up and brayed. We all watched the boy walk away and disappear out of sight.

"Well, Eddie," Pa said, "I guess we'd better figure out how to get this big boy home."

Pa handed me one of the lead ropes and, together, we led the jackass out of the pen. As we walked him out of the big barn, Pa was quiet. I knew he was sorry to take the boy's pet jackass, but he'd paid the money and the animal was now his.

We led Samson to the truck and slid down the ramp in the

back. Pa was looking a tad skeptical whether the big jackass would fit in the truck, but we was bound to give it a try.

I saw Bobby Ray come toward us with a man I took to be his father. Pa had the same thought and held out his hand to shake. Once they'd shook hands, the man held out his hand to me, so I stepped up and shook his hand, too.

"I'm Bob James, Bobby Ray's dad," he explained though we already thought it was the case.

"Bobby Ray said you bought Samson, so I wanted to drop over and tell you a few things about him before you head off to home."

"Why, I appreciate that, Mr. James," Pa answered and looked expectant.

"Well, Samson is a good stud jack, but that also means he can be a handful. Bobby Ray here is about the only one he's taken to. I was sorry we had to sell him, but you know how times are gettin' hard. I can't afford to keep more'n one jackass and we've also got General Lee back home. He's the senior jack and I couldn't see lettin' him go."

"Samson did show his spunk, I'll admit, but he seems to be quiet enough now."

"Oh, sure, he's good as long as there ain't no mares in the area. Just be careful when you bring in the mares 'cause he might get a little crazy. He ain't mean, just real enthused about his job, I'd say." The man chuckled a bit at his own joke.

"I already promised Bobby Ray we'd take good care of him,

and I shook his hand on it. That's my solemn word," Pa said as he looked at Bobby Ray to see if he understood what he was saying. Bobby Ray nodded his head to show he knew he and Pa had a gentlemen's agreement.

"Well, that's about it," Mr. James said, looking as if it were time for him to leave. "But, we could help you load him up."

"That'd be right nice of you. You know, in case you come down our way, we live a little ways outside Hereford. Perkins is the name. You can ask anybody where to find us."

"We just might do that," Mr. James said.

We loaded up Samson easy enough and drove off.

"I think we'll call him Bucephalus," Pa said as we were driving home.

"Why not just call him Samson, Pa? That's his name."

"He's got a new life now, so he should have a new name. Besides, I always wanted to call a horse Bucephalus, but I think a jack can live up to the name just fine." We ended up just calling him Beau, 'cause it's a lot easier to say.

Out of the Chicken Coop

Most animals on the farm were there for a purpose, rarely as pets. That meant that animals were not allowed in the house like they are today. If they got in, however, it wasn't always easy to get them out again.

WHEN I WAS just a little kid, no more'n seven if I remember rightly, I was down in the chicken yard tossin' grain like I was tol'. This one little red hen started followin' me around instead of peckin' up the grain like the other chickens. I thought it strange, but just went about my business.

When I opened up the gate to leave, the red hen just whooshed right through 'fore I could get it closed. I tol' her, "Now you get back in there," and opened the gate just a bit for her. She didn't pay any mind to the invite, but just headed on across the yard as fast as two feet could take her.

I latched up the gate and took off after her. I thought I'd better grab her before she got up to the porch. Ma doesn't like chickens on the porch 'cause of the mess they make. So, I was runnin' after the hen and she was makin' a bee-line for the house.

Well, she was faster 'n me, so she beat me handy and up on the porch she went. The kitchen door was open to let the heat out since Ma was bakin' pies. That hen just traipsed right in like she'd come to visit. I caught up with her finally and she and me went round the kitchen table a time or two. I was glad Ma wasn't there 'cause I know that hen wouldn't of lasted two seconds if that were the case. I figured I'd better catch the chicken 'fore Ma turned her into supper.

It were a standoff. I'd go right around the table, and the hen'd go left. I'd go left, and she'd go right. When I stopped, she stopped. Mostly, chickens don't have much sense, which is why people don't take to them much. Except for eatin' and eggs, of course. But, I was beginnin' to think this was one smart chicken.

I'd left the kitchen door open so's I could chase the chicken out, but that just perked up Ol' Spot's curiosity as he come in to see what was up. Of course, Ma don't allow no dogs in the kitchen, neither, so I'd two strikes again' me already.

The hen didn't care for Spot bein' in the kitchen, neither. That's one thing Ma and the hen would agree on. So, she gave out a couple of clucks and jumped up on a chair, which was shoved under the table. So, I got down on my hands and knees and crawled under the table. Spot thought this was a good idea, so he come under, too.

The hen spied Spot and Spot spied the hen and there was a

lot less room under there after that. Spot jumped at the hen and she jumped over to another chair and Spot just followed her under the table. He'd pretty much forgot I was there, too, so he scrunched his way right over the top of me, pushin' me flat to the floor. The hen's jumpin' from one chair to the next and Spot was runnin' around in circles trying to catch her.

Cluck, cluck, bark, bark. I was surprised Ma hadn't already showed up.

I decided there weren't enough room for me, Spot, and the chicken, so I started to crawl out. But, that didn't work so well, as Spot lunged at the chicken just as I was pushin' out from under the table.

Now, Spot wasn't a real big dog, but he weighed in about thirty pounds and was plenty strong. When he jumped up to catch the chicken, he knocked me over and I rolled up against the leg of the table. Yep, that's the same leg needing fixin' for the last month and Pa hadn't got to it. It's not surprisin' the leg pushed away when I rolled up against it. That end of the table fell on my back and all the pies slid off on the floor. It was pretty startlin', so I'll admit I yelped some. Course, Spot was barkin' and the hen was a-cluckin' so it was gettin' right noisy in there.

When the side of the table fell, I could see the hen kind of squirt out the other side and make for the door. Spot scrabbled out and hit the floor runnin' after her. I'd just crawled out from under the table and, wouldn't you know, Ma showed up and was standin' there like she does with her fists balled up on her hips. She'd got that look, I'm sorry to say. I 'spect you know the one I'm talkin' about. Her eyes were kind of narrowed down and her mouth wasn't smilin' at all.

I stood there in front of her tryin' to think of what to say, but nothin' good was comin' to mind. So, I just tol' the truth.

"Ma, it was the chicken. And Spot, he was chasin' the chicken. It weren't my fault."

"I don't see no chicken and I don't see no Spot, neither."

I looked around at the table all cockeyed and the door opened, and she was right. Spot and the hen headed for other parts, leavin' me with the blame. Even at the tender age of seven, I knew the next step was a trip to the woodshed and a switchin'.

Ma took hold of my suspenders and walked me out the door.

"But, Ma . . ." I thought maybe whinin' might help, but it didn't.

I thought I was doomed for sure, but then I saw Spot standin' by the chicken house barkin' to beat all. Ma noticed too, and her hand eased up on my suspenders just a bit.

"That red hen got outta the coop and went to the kitchen. I was just tryin' to get her out an' Spot come in and he made the table fall down."

Ma let go of my suspenders and stopped in the middle of the yard. She looked at Spot by the chicken coop and she spotted the red hen stuck between the coop and the pig pen.

"All right, you're let off this time, but don't you go chasin' the chickens into my kitchen no more," she said. She turned about and went back to the house. I headed to the chicken coop and pulled Spot's collar 'til he backed off. I opened the coop gate and the little red hen, waitin' for her chance, ran like a house afire back into the pen. I slammed the gate behind her. I guessed she'd had enough fun for one day.

"You don't be comin' outta the pen no more," I told her stern-like. It didn't do no good, though. The next week she got out again. And the week after that. I don't think there was any keepin' that little hen in the coop once she'd been out. Finally, Ma just let her stay since it was just too much trouble tryin' to keep her out.

I guess that's the way of any critter. They like to run around as they please. I could understand it, as that's what I liked, too.

Pa's Story

World War I took many young men away from their homes and sent them off to foreign shores. Eddie's Pa was one of those young men. He has his own tale to tell.

IN 1916, I was still a young buck and not yet married, so I signed up with Black Jack Pershing to go after Pancho Villa. Ol' Pancho and his banditos came into US territory and killed a bunch of folks in Columbus, New Mexico.

I was real good with horses, so soon I was the veterinarian. This was just as well, as I didn't take well to using a gun. I'd never studied vetting in school, but I'd grown up on a farm in Nebraska and knew just about all there was to know about horses and mules. We chased Pancho and his gang just about all over Mexico, but never did catch up with him. A couple years later, I was still in the service, so I ended up goin' to France with Black Jack when he got to be a General. I could have decided not to go as I'd done my time, but I knew Black Jack could put me to good use.

We were on the troop ship for weeks. Everybody was

seasick for the first few days. The horses seemed to fare fine in that regard, but I was worried we couldn't exercise them enough. We brought them up from the hold, a few at a time, and let them stretch their legs. We'd lead them in a quick walk around the deck. With the metal decks, we didn't want them to move very fast for fear they'd slip and fall. I'd hate to have to put down a horse with a broken leg, so we took it real easy. As a result, the horses were not in good fightin' shape by the time we landed in France.

It took some time, but me and Joe, who got assigned to be my assistant, got them in shape again. Mostly the horses were used to pack gear, but a few officers still rode them. Black Jack Pershing liked to ride on occasion, as did Captain Patton. I thought we should only have mules, since they make better pack animals than horses, but there were never enough mules to go around.

We weren't in too many battles directly as we were the supply line for the army, but in 1918 it turned pretty bad when we went into the Argonne Forest. They called this an 'offensive.' I can see why as it offended me a lot. The fighting went on for nearly two months and only ended in November when the big guys signed the Treaty at Versailles.

In that short two months, it was hell on earth. Thousands of men died. One whole division, the 77th, was cut off for near a week and held out surrounded by the German forces. It was some battle, I can tell you. Almost all day long, I could hear the shells bursting and the sharp reports of rifle fire. And I heard the screams of dying men and horses.

The worst part for me was the horses being swept up in the middle of the battle. It broke my heart to go out on the fields after the fighting passed by and after the dead and wounded men were collected. Sometimes the ground was so soaked with blood that my boots were covered before I got back. A horse with an artery torn open bleeds gallons of blood; men only a few pints. It angered me when I thought how much the horses gave. They didn't even have a say in goin' to war. Men, at least, had a choice.

I carried a sidearm and had to shoot more horses than I can count. Those we could save, we'd bring back to the line and see if we could treat their wounds. It was a second heartbreak when they wouldn't heal proper and we'd take them out behind the tents to put them down. We dug a deep trench to bury them for health reasons and we kept digging every day to hold them all.

While we treated the horses, close by we could see the wounded men being brought back from the battlefield. Legs and arms were already gone or had to be cut off by the doctors right there in the field. From the history I'd read about the Civil War, this was just about as bad. If the choice was amputate or die, then they had to do what was necessary. We dug another trench to hold the arms and legs the doctors cut off; the dead soldiers we wrapped in oilcloth to be sent back behind the lines, where we hoped to send their bodies back home to their families.

All told I spent twenty months in France. It was the worst part of my life and I hoped and prayed we'd never see another war like this again.

§ § §

Pa's story made me sad in a way, though I was proud of him for what he did in the war. It seemed like people would learn to get along. I never was sure why Pa had to go to France. Later in my own life, I'd learn what it was to go to war. I was lucky to not go overseas, but somethin' in me wished I had.

The Corn Patch Incident

Barn raising is a community affair that takes place in almost all rural societies across the country. In Texas, nearly every community event also includes a barbecue, although it's sometimes by default. It all depends on why the barn needs raising.

A LITTLE TORNADO came through last week and Nate Simmons' barn got flattened. Specially bad for Mr. Simmons, two cows were in the barn at the time and didn't make it out alive. All it meant was there was plenty of meat for a barbecue when all the neighbors came around to rebuild the barn.

The cows got butchered right away and Mr. Simmons managed to sell quite a bit, but there was still a good half left over for the barbecue. My Pa and me went to help set up a pit. It takes a couple of days to roast a proper half, so Mr. Simmons got it fired up on Thursday. By Saturday it was pretty much ready to go.

All the neighbors gathered up their tools and their families. We packed up and headed over to Mr. Simmons along with everybody else. Mr. Simmons brought in a load of lumber so everybody just brought their tools. We got there in the mornin' and the men made good progress on clearin' the scrap from the old barn and startin' to frame up the new one. They salvaged what they could, stackin' the good lumber to one side. They built some rough tables from a few pieces that wouldn't be any good for the barn. Of course, people brought along chairs and such as they knew folks would need some place to sit come meal time.

The ladies, bein' warned, already baked up biscuits and pies. More'n one family brought a kettle full of beans or potatoes ready to serve. They set those around the fire pit to keep warm while the work of barn raisin' was in progress. I helped by carryin' tools and boards to the men as they worked. It got pretty noisy what with all the poundin' and sawin' goin' on.

Along about noon, we could smell the beef pretty good and it made my mouth water. Ma called me over and handed me a gunny sack.

"You go fetch corn, Eddie. We'll need mebbe fifty ears so don't come back without that many."

"Yes'm, Ma. Can I take along Sister? She can pick the low ears while I get the high ones."

"Sure enough. She's gettin' big enough to carry her weight," Ma said then she went back to stirrin' the kettles sittin' next to the pit.

I grabbed Sister, who's really Dorothy, but we called her Sister. Anyways, we took off to the corn field and proceeded to pull the ripe ears off the stalks. It takes the right eye to get the ripe ones. Some folks have to peel back the silk from the ear and take a look. Me and Sister had done this so many times, we could tell just by how fat the ear looked. So, we were movin' along pretty good and had about half the ears Ma said to get.

I looked down the row to see how far we'd got when I saw a skunk traipsin' up toward me. First off, I wondered what the little polecat was doin' out in the middle of the day. Most often, they hunt at night. I stopped quick and looked around to see where Sister was. I couldn't see her, so I decided just to let her know.

"Hey, Sister. There's a skunk up here, so don't go up the row no more," I yelled.

"What row, Eddie?" she hollered back.

"The row I'm on," I answered and wondered why she couldn't have figured that out herself.

"Which row, I say-ed?" she asked again, soundin' a little disgusted now.

"This darn row!" Why didn't the fool girl know which row I was on? Then, it occurred to me I didn't know where she was neither.

"Say somethin' again and I'll find you."

"I'm heeere!" she sang out.

I could tell she was in front of me and a row or two south. I looked back to where the skunk was, but he'd disappeared. It came to me she might be close to where the skunk was by this time.

"Look out for the skunk," I called out.

"What skunk?"

Sometimes I wondered if she thought anything out. "The skunk I said was up in front of me," I said a bit on the mad side now.

Then I heard the scream from Sister and I figured she'd found the skunk. I dropped the sack of corn and ducked through the corn row. Sister ran smack into me. I saw the skunk no more'n five feet up the row. He was stampin' his feet and hissin' to beat the band. They do that afore they spray. Then, he raised up on its front legs, rear-end pointin' right at us. He was fixin' to shoot!

I grabbed Sister by the arm and jumped through the row back the way I'd come. I pulled her through just in time as I could smell the skunk had let loose. I grabbed up the sack and we both hightailed it up the row in the opposite direction as the skunk.

We ain't gone more than a couple of steps when we see another skunk in front of us. Then another! We was bein' overrun with skunks. I dropped the bag of corn as it was slowin' me down. Sister and me jumped through to the next row and looked both ways to see if any more skunks were headed our way. We didn't see none, so we skedaddled back out of the cornfield. When we got to the end, we stopped to think over our situation some.

"Ma won't be none too happy we didn't bring back the corn," Sister said, pointing out the obvious.

"Well, I don't want to go back in there," I answered, thinkin' fast as I knew Sister was right. Skunk smell or a lickin'? Not much of a choice, so I decided we'd go back in for the corn.

"C'mon, then. We gotta go back and get the corn."

"Nooo, I'm not goin'," Sister got her stubborn voice and I knew it wouldn't do any good to argue with her.

"All right, but I'm goin' tell Ma you didn't help," I answered knowin' it was the only thing that might change her mind.

"She didn't say I had to go, she just said I could go. Eddie, you're not goin' to put this off on me." With that, she swung herself around to march off. I grabbed her shoulder and her braids whipped around and hit me in the face. It didn't bother me, though. I was gettin' desperate, after all.

"Ow!" she yelled and kicked me in the shins. I was glad I wore my boots so it didn't hurt much.

"I'm sorry, I'm sorry. I just need your help," I whined some so she'd feel sorry for me.

We both stood there for awhile lookin' at the corn patch, tryin' to decide how we'd go about gettin' in and out.

"What if we just pick the corn on the edge here?" Sister asked.

"No good. The stalks out here don't have much good corn.

We'd never get fifty ears."

We continued to stand there starin' at the patch, hopin' something would come to mind.

"We'll just have to go in," I finally decided and squared myself up to the task.

Once we'd decided–although Sister still looked like she'd bolt–we headed back into the corn. Our best move was to get the sack as it already had half the corn we needed. So, we started down the row where I'd dropped it.

I didn't see any sign of the skunk, so I was hopin' she was gone. I figured the others to be her pups, since skunks are usually loners. It was no wonder she was in a fightin' mood as I was between her and her children. Any mother would be het up.

We got the sack with no further trouble, filled it up, and headed back to the barbecue pit. Ma saw us comin' and waved us to put the sack by some big kettles with water heatin' up. As soon as the water started to boil, then we'd drop the ears in. But, I knew our job wasn't finished as we also had to husk the corn.

I saw my friend Red watchin' the men work, so I called him over to help. We got the ears shucked in no time at all. He did notice one small problem.

"This corn stinks, Eddie. Where didja get it?" he asked whilst holdin' his nose with one hand and tryin' to shuck with the other.

"We ran into a skunk," I answered a mite testily as he didn't have to go in the corn patch and didn't have no right to complain.

Sister didn't answer him, but she did punch him in the arm. That's generally her way of dealin' with a complainer.

The water was startin' to boil, so we threw the ears in, dividin' them between the two big kettles. Ma saw we were puttin' the corn in, so she came over to check our work. She's particular about shuckin' and doesn't like if we leave too much silk on the cobs.

As she got near us, she started wrinklin' her nose and I knew she was smellin' the skunk, too.

"What in tarnation happened to this corn?" she asked, glarin' at me and Sister.

"Ma, it ain't our fault. There was a skunk in the corn. Matter of fact, there were five skunks in the corn. We jus' didn't get away in time. We were lucky it didn't hit us, too." I ran out the excuses, so just shut my mouth.

Ma stood there lookin' down her nose at us with her arms crossed. Her glasses were glintin' in the sun so I couldn't see her eyes, but I figured what they looked like. I'd seen that look often enough to know.

"You two, and you Red, go back to the corn field and get up another fifty ears," she pronounced our sentence.

Glumly, I grabbed the bag, but Ma took it away and tossed it in the pit where it lit up and was gone in a flash. She grabbed up another bag and handed it over.

The skunks seemed to have left the territory, so we had no more problems. We got up another bag of corn, shucked it, and threw it in the fresh pots of water Ma put to boilin'. Our previous bunch o' corn went in the pit. The ears burned slower than the bag since the corn was fresh, so to speak.

After it was all said and done, though, it was a good barbecue and we finished up the barn by dusk. Everybody headed home weary, but glad they could help out a neighbor in need. That's just the way it worked around these parts. Sister and me were just glad we escaped the skunks in the corn patch.

Moonlight Ride

Death is always a part of life and that was never more true than during the Depression. People lived, and died, out on the Texas prairies sometimes with nobody around to watch them pass.

DOROTHY and me grew up on a farm in west Texas. It was six hundred forty acres, which is the size most farms were in that part of the country. To tell the truth, I'd rather we owned a ranch with longhorn steers, but six-hundred-forty acres  was only room enough for crops, not cattle. Still, Sister and me had our horses. We rode to school, we rode to town, we rode all over the prairie. Naturally, we got to be pretty good riders.

We had neighbors to visit. Mrs. Garner was one. She was the widow lady one farm east of us. At night, we could look across and see the lights in her farmhouse. She was by herself since her husband took the flu in 1918 and died. I wasn't born yet, but I'd heard it was pretty bad in the big cities where people live right next to each other. It wasn't so bad out in the west where there's a little space between neighbors, but some folk still got the flu and died.

Mrs. Garner didn't actually do the work on her place. For a share of the crop, some Mexicans offered to do the work durin' planting and harvesting time. In between, she was by herself. But, she wasn't always alone as there was church to go to and socials and such going on. Lots of the town ladies came out to visit her and she did the same with them.

In December, the crops were already in so there wasn't much to do. One night, we were just sitting around in front of the fire doing our homework. It was getting late, so Pa went out on the porch to smoke his cigar before bedtime. Ma didn't like the smell, so she didn't let him smoke inside. He came back in and whispered sumpin to Ma. She went out on the porch for a bit, then she come back herself. They whispered some more.

"Eddie," Pa said to me, "I want you to go saddle up Brownie and take a ride over to Mrs. Garner's place."

"Why's that, Pa?" I asked him.

"Oh, no special reason. I'd just like you to go check up on her. Her lights are still on and she's usually not up this late."

"Sure, Pa."

I didn't mind a little moonlight ride, so I hustled on out to the barn and saddled up Brownie. When I was all ready, I led him up to the house and Pa was waiting there with a kerosene lantern. I mounted up and Pa handed me up the light. Ma came out and gave me a bag.

"Just tell her we thought she'd like some leftover

cornbread," she said pointing to the bag. I thought it pretty strange to be deliverin' cornbread at ten o'clock at night, but it wasn't up to me to question.

I started out across the prairie, going slow so Brownie could see his way and not step in a hole. Horses got real good vision at night, so you can always trust 'em to find their own way.

The moon shone down on the frost forming on the ground. Lookin' across to Mrs. Garner's, I thought it a beautiful sight. The frost and the big moon hangin' close to the horizon looked like a postcard picture. I thought it was real pretty, though boys aren't supposed to think of such things.

When I got to her place I saw the only light was in the kitchen, so I went round the other side of the house to knock on the door. When I come up to the door, I looked through the glass and saw her down on the kitchen floor. I started to pound on the door, but she didn't move and that got me worried.

I tried the doorknob and it wasn't locked so I went in. I don't know why, but I thought I needed to be quiet so I went close to her and whispered "Mrs. Garner, are you alive?" Thinkin' back, that was a pretty stupid thing to say, 'cause I don't think she would've been alayin' there if she was alive.

She didn't move. I'd seen lots of dead animals in my time, and I was pretty sure she was dead, too. There's something about a dead critter that's different from one just asleep. All that come to my mind was they're too still, like a rock or a piece of wood. Something leaves the body and it ain't no more than a thing when it's dead.

I went back out and got up on Brownie. I left the lantern and cornbread on the porch so I could get back home quicker. I told Pa and he shook his head with a sad look in his eyes.

"She was getting old," he said. "She must've been close to seventy." With that, he put on his heavy coat and got himself ready to walk back over to her place.

"Do you want to ride Brownie, Pa?"

"No, son, but thanks for offering. You go put up Brownie, then you and Sister ought to go on to bed."

"Yessir," me and Dorothy said. She headed for the sleeping loft and me for the barn.

When I did get to bed, I couldn't get to sleep for a long time. I kept thinking of that poor old woman, all alone in her farmhouse and it made me sad. I decided I never wanted to be alone like that and die all by myself, out on the prairie with nobody by my side.

The Bone Hunters

Between 1870 and 1937, the bone business played a major role in the economy of Texas. In the nineteenth century, the bones were from the millions of buffalo slaughtered for their hides and then left to rot on the plains. Once the buffalo were depleted, cattle became the primary source of bones. During the Great Depression, hundreds of families overcame droughts, debts, and famine by picking up and selling bones. Bone buyers made a circuit of the farms, collecting tons of bones to be ground to meal, leached of calcium phosphate to fire the furnaces of bone china makers, and made into buttons for the garment factories.

In 1929, at the age of nineteen, James Ridgley Whiteman discovered the existence of Clovis Man, believed at that time to be the earliest human being to live on the North American continent.

"HEY, YOU DROP that right now!" I yelled at my little sister when I saw her pickin' up a cowpie. Cowpies was fine, if they were good and dry, but the one Dorothy picked up looked a mite green.

"Girls, they don't have no sense," I muttered under my breath. I didn't want her to hear me or she'd get all grumpy.

I'd only let her come along 'cause she kept beggin' over and over until I had to say yes. She saw I was making money from the bones and she thought she'd like to make some, too. Only trouble was she kept gettin' distracted. For awhile, all she'd do is pick wildflowers, and now cowpies, for gosh sakes.

The pile of bones we'd collected was gettin' pretty high behind the barn. I figured the bone buyer ought to be comin' round again soon. It'd been near four weeks, and the man drove his route pretty regular. I reckoned I'd get close to two dollars for that pile.

Me and my sister Dorothy, who we call Sister, were spending the summer of 1930 with a cousin of our Pa's down in Bailey County, just a stone's throw, well, about ten miles, southeast of Clovis, New Mexico.

The family, name of Porter, ran a small ranch where they raised some cattle. I thought it'd be a grand adventure, since I always wished I could be a cowboy. So, when Pa said we'd be visiting the Porters, I was pretty happy, but the Porter herd counted only five head of cows, and them being milk cows to boot. Of course, the reason we was here was not too good neither. My littlest sister, Mary Ada, took sick and Ma had too much to handle with that. So, me and Sister was sent off to stay with our cousins for a while.

Still, me and Sister were tryin' to make the best of it. When I learned we could make some money collectin' bones, the two of us spent just about every day riding our horses out on the plains. We'd made up a travois just like the Indians used. I cut two saplings, after askin' of course, and trimmed all the small twigs off, then tied them together with some rope about a third of the way from one end. I tied it loose, so the saplings could be spread apart at the long end. Then, I spread an old blanket across and strapped it down to each sapling. It was meant to cross over the horse's back at the short end, with the long ends draggin' behind.

When it was all ready it looked kind of like a flat teepee laid over the horse with the small end up over the withers. With a travois, we could load up a lot more bones than if we tried to carry them atop the horse. Sister could sit between the saplings where they started to spread, so we could still travel pretty fast.

We headed generally west, crisscrossing up to five miles north and south of the dirt road headin' into Clovis. We looked in draws, in particular, cause cows tended to take their dyin' steps to get as close to water as they could. Unfortunate for the cows, cause most often the draw was dry and the poor cow just died of thirst. Bad for the cow, but good for two kids lookin' to make their fortune collectin' bones.

We'd been at it for a while and had pretty much cleared out everything to be found almost into New Mexico. One morning, we folded up the travois and carried it along, making fast tracks over the New Mexico border. I wasn't exactly sure when we crossed the state line, since there was no sign or anything, but I could make a pretty good guess at it.

Now that we were in fresh bone pickin' territory, I rigged up the travois again and started searching for the draws most likely to have cow bones

We'd been at this for a couple of hours, when I spotted a man drivin' a Model T right out in the middle of the plains. There weren't no road, so he was goin' along pretty slow and I could see him bouncin' around quite a bit. I thought this was pretty interestin', so we stopped and waited for the man to drive our way. Dorothy and me waved to get the man's attention and, soon enough, the Model T pulled right up to us. We held the horses tight since that car was plenty noisy. The man turned off the ignition, the car coughed a couple of times before it died.

"Howdy," I said and tipped my hat like Ma taught me. Sister just raised her hand in a little wave.

"Howdy, back at ya,'" the man answered. He wasn't dressed like a town man, but not like a cowboy neither. He wore tan-colored clothes that looked like they were made for workin'. His hat was almost, but not quite a cowboy hat. I thought I'd seen that kind of hat before. The man was only twenty or so, but he looked kind of rough like he spent a lot of time out in the sun. His clothes were dusty and wrinkled, but not like a bum. Besides, a bum wouldn't have a car, now would he?

"I'm Ridge Whiteman," the man said thumbin' his chest.

"I'm Eddie and that's my little sister, Dorothy," I said. Now that introductions were done, maybe we could find out what the man was doin' way out here, but he beat me to it.

"What are you kids up to?"

"We're huntin' bones," I answered.

"Oh? I hunt bones, too. What do you do with the bones you find?"

"We sell 'em to the bone buyer. What do you do with your bones?"

"I hope they'll be put in a museum," the man replied.

I took a squint at the few bones in our travois. "What bones are you findin'?"

"Mammoth bones."

I couldn't help but laugh. Mammoths were those big, hairy elephants runnin' around these parts about a million years ago.

The man laughed, too. "Eddie," he said, " I'm serious. Just last year I found some and, the most exciting thing is that I found some arrowheads stuck in them."

"Just where was this?" I was suspicious that the man was just making fun of me.

"Blackwater Draw. It's just a couple of miles that way," the man replied pointing toward the west.

"Look, I can see maybe you're not believing me," he continued, "so I'd like to prove it. You two just stake out your horses here. We'll take a quick drive over and I'll show you."

This was an offer that got my attention. I looked at Sister and she shrugged. Whatever I wanted, she was tellin' me.

"Well, if it's only a couple of miles, we can just ride over," I said eying the beat up Model T. Much as we loved to go with Pa and Ma in the truck, this car didn't look none too safe to me.

"Suit yourself. I don't drive too fast out here anyway, so it won't be hard to keep up." The man hopped out and gave the crank a couple of turns, carefully pulling down so it wouldn't kick back, and the motor started right up. He jumped fast to get back into the car, let off the handbrake, and eased out the clutch.

While Mr. Whiteman was starting the car, me and Sister took the travois off her horse and stuck the poles into a couple of prairie dog holes so they'd stand up. It'd be easier to find when we came back this way. I boosted Sister up on her horse, then jumped up on my own and we took out after the Model T.

Moving along at an easy lope, we soon caught up with Mr. Whiteman and just rode alongside the car as it bounced over the sage-scattered flat lands. It wasn't too long before we came up to the edge of a deep draw and Mr. Whiteman pulled right up to the rim where he stopped and let the Model T die again.

We got down off the horses, and dropped the reins to ground tie them. The horses knew what was expected and immediately started nosing around for any grass to graze on. They wouldn't go far with the reins on the ground.

"Come along down here," Mr. Whiteman started down a goat trail leading down the rocky side of the draw. As we scooted and slipped down the trail, I could see the walls were layered rock. This was pretty normal for a draw. As the water washed down them, the walls were dug away and you could see where layers of dirt formed up and turned to rock over the years—thousands of years. I did recall a lesson at school on the geology of Texas and learned about some of this.

Soon, we reached the bottom and Mr. Whiteman led us a few dozen feet along the wall. Some of the rock wall was chipped away and pieces were laying on the floor of the draw.

"Here," Mr. Whiteman pointed and I was amazed to see the shape of a leg bone, but it was bigger'n any bone I'd ever seen. I figured he wasn't puttin' me on since a real mammoth bone was right in front of my own two eyes. I looked at Sister, but she was busy picking wildflowers again and didn't pay any mind.

The man pulled a small hammer from his belt and started tapping around the mammoth bone.

"Look, here," he pointed and, sure enough, I could make out an arrow head. Little chips were knocked off along the edge to make it sharp. "That's called fluting," he explained when he saw me runnin' my finger along the chipped edge of the arrowhead.

"This is really sumthin'," I said quietly. I hardly knew what to say, I was so flabbergasted I actually got to touch real mammoth bones.

"These bones, and that arrowhead, are thousands of years old. I found them last year and I sent pictures and some of the material to a professor at the Smithsonian. He thought what I sent was good enough they'll come out soon for a real archeology dig." Mr. Whiteman stood back up straight and looked mighty proud of himself.

I thought he should be proud. It was really special to find mammoth bones, but the fact that an arrowhead was stuck into the bone was even better. Mr. Whiteman explained how scientists found mammoth remains before so they knew they'd ranged around here about eleven thousand years before. What was never been found before was proof that humans were here at the same time as the mammoths.

"It's not for sure yet. I'll have to wait for the Smithsonian dig to make sure, but I'm thinking I've got really good proof."

"Yessir," I looked up at the young man with some respect. I was only a kid, but even I could figure out this was pretty exciting stuff. Maybe I'd like to be an archeologist instead of a cowboy. After all, archeologists got to collect bigger bones.

Finally, we climbed back up the goat path. Me and Sister mounted up and waved goodbye as we rode back to where we'd left the travois. When I decided we'd go bone hunting, I never expected to find mammoth bones. But now I'd seen 'em, so I could truthfully say we hunted for a mammoth and caught up with one in Blackwater Draw.

Ma Yote and Her Cubs

Besides rattlesnakes and jackrabbits, the farmers and ranchers considered coyotes to be vermin. If the prairie wolves made the mistake of entering the world of people, they would be killed whether or not they'd actually done any harm.

I LIKED TO catch horny toads on occasion and keep them in a glass cannin' jar, which Ma lets me do so long as I clean up good afterwards. I'd scoop up some sand and dirt into the jar and a couple of good sized rocks for  them to sit on. I laid the jar sideways so's they could stretch out to rest. I learned what bugs they liked by feedin' 'em lots of different kinds. If they started to look peaked, I'd let 'em go, elsewise I'd keep 'em for a week or so. If you're a city slicker, then I'll tell you that a horny toad ain't a toad at all. It's a flat, fat lizard with a rough hide and a ruff of spikes 'round its neck like a lace collar, which some ladies, but not Ma, wore to dress up.

Bein's it was a fine day, I took a walk to the sandstone canyon that runs near our farm. In the summer, it gives up a good stock of lizards and horny toads. I always hoped to find a horny toad, but there be plenty of other interestin' lizards, too. The schoolhouse has a big book of critters by some scientist. I'll admit that the man knew his stuff, even if he lived back east. I'd look up what I found in his book so I'd know next time if I spotted the same kind again.

Anyways, the canyon starts out on one end real shallow and gets deeper as it runs west. It ends up runnin' into a bluff that turns it into a box canyon. Through spring, it had water in the deep end, but by high summer it was all dried out. I'd walk down it from the shallow end, keepin' my eyes peeled on the walls where the critters lived. This particular day was frustratin' 'cause I didn't see a single thing until I got near the end.

I stopped dead in my tracks. Three of the cutest little coyote cubs you'd hope to meet were rompin' around near the end of the canyon. I looked every which way for their mama, but didn't see her. I suspected she might be out lookin' for dinner.

The cubs looked my way, but didn't spook. They just looked interested for a bit, then they went back to bitin' each other's tails. I had to grin at the squeaky lil' growls they let out as they played at huntin'.

I sat down partly hid by a big boulder no more'n twenty feet from 'em just to watch. I commenced to thinkin' that I might catch one of the cubs and raise him up like a dog. Coyotes looked like dogs, but I'd never heard of anyone who brought one home. I decided I'd try to tame one of the cubs, but I'd wait until their ma weaned them. They'd still be small enough for me to wrangle, but not so big as to be dangerous.

Somethin' moved atop the canyon wall and caught my eye. Mama Coyote hung her head over the edge and bared her teeth. Even from twenty feet up I could hear the growling. I stood up slow and commenced to backin' away. She jumped down and I nearly fell on my behind. I don't know to this day how she done it, but that coyote found footholds to scramble down that rock wall what looked like a lizard might not get a grip.

She hit the bottom lickety-split, so I backed up a mite faster. Not too fast, or I knew she'd come after me. Lucky for me, she weren't inclined to do that, so I turned around and took off. I kept alookin' over my shoulder, but she stayed with her cubs, sniffin' them to make sure they were alright. In that way, she reminded me of my own ma. She can sound mean enough to shake you right outta yer boots, but I know it's generally for my own good.

I went home and found Pa in the barn pitchin' hay. I told him about the cubs, and my plan to make one of them a pet. He kiboshed that idea plenty quick.

"Eddie, I'm surprised at you. I thought I taught you better."

I hung my head, 'cause I know he did tell me to leave wild animals alone. But I forgot. "Yessir, Pa." I thought a second. "But can I go watch 'em? I promise I won't bother 'em none."

Pa leaned on the pitchfork handle, holding it 'tween his hands. "You can do that, but I'll go with you."

"I don't want you to bother yourself none," I said back real quick. I figured I could watch the cubs for an hour or two each day, dependin' on the presence of their ma.

"That's okay. I'll go just the once to look the situation over.

I'll take the rifle in case. I won't even go down the canyon with you."

I almost yelled at Pa, "You wouldn't shoot 'em!"

Pa put his hand on my shoulder to calm me down. "Of course not. But you need to know that some other farmer 'round here might kill them. The coyotes go after the lambs in the spring, and that costs the farmers their livelihood."

"Like the jackrabbits and rattlesnakes?"

"Exactly like that. We don't like to kill the critters, but sometimes it's necessary."

"Yessir, Pa." I moved to leave, but Pa caught my arm.

"We'll go tomorrow first thing. If the mother hunts in the morning, you got a better chance of observin' the cubs without her being a danger to you."

I skipped out of the barn, and went off to feed the chickens, which was my chore and I hadn't done it yet. Ma would give me a lickin' if I didn't get it done soon.

Next morning, Pa loaded his rifle and we walked to the canyon entrance. I continued on down the the slope while he walked along the top. When we got near the end, I couldn't see the cubs. I looked up at Pa. "Do you see the coyotes up there?" He shook his head, and I trusted his word since he was lookin' all directions.

I admit I was disappointed. I'd probably chased off the ma coyote 'cause I got too close to her cubs. She most likely packed up and moved away. I huffed out a big breath. I jus' wanted to watch the cubs for awhile. I waved at Pa. He waved back and hollered, "I'll see you at home." Then he disappeared away from the cliff top.

I was just about to turn around, when I saw a glint of something a few feet ahead. I looked closer. A pair of red eyes starin' out at me from a hole in the rocks. Mama Coyote had a den! I sat down behind the big boulder to watch a piece. 'For long, one of the cubs come venturin' out of the little cave, and the other two soon followed along. My lips like to split my grin was so big. The coyotes hadn't moved on after all!

I came back every couple of days. Sometimes the cubs were out playin', sometimes Ma Yote, which is what I called her, warned me off. I took to bringin' some jerky with me. I tossed a piece a few feet in front of my rock. She slunk up a bit, her nose workin' the air. I could tell she knew I'd put out somethin' good.

When I come back the next day, the jerky was gone, but I couldn't tell if Ma Yote got it or some varmint. 'Course, I didn't think of the coyotes as varmints, even if all the farmers did. Once I got to know 'em, they was my friends. At least I hoped that was the case.

I threw out some more jerky. Mama Yote came no more'n ten feet from me and picked up that piece quick like and run it back to her cubs. My chest swelled up like to burst, and I grinned ear to ear. Each time I tossed a chunk, she'd come and fetch it.

I figured at this rate, I'd have her eatin' right out of my hand. Or maybe the cubs would come close to get their own share. I still had a plan, just in case mind you, that I'd make one of them cubs mine. I'd warrant that Pa wouldn't like it, but I think he'd come 'round 'ventually.

Then one day I went up to check the little guys and found two of the cubs dead. Ma Yote and the other cub were nowhere around. Each of the cubs had a clean bullet hole in their sides right over their hearts. Blood matted the soft fuzz of their baby coats. Some farmer had come in and killed 'em.

My face went all red and hot. Why did they need to go an' kill little babies? It weren't fair. The coyotes were just bein' coyotes. Besides, Pa had said that they didn't eat livestock as a rule, but went after mice and rabbits. I couldn't see any cause for them to be killed.

I wiped my eyes on my shirt sleeve, then carried the cubs to their cave. Their bodies were limp and heavy. They smelled just like regular puppies, 'cept for the blood. I piled rocks in front to keep out the varmints. That's all I could do for them.

After I sat a spell, I went home and tol' Pa. He said, "You knew it might happen, Eddie. Farmers have to protect their livestock."

That didn't ease my mind at all. To this day, it makes me mad and sad that those little cubs got kilt for no reason. I think of how Ma Yote felt when she come home and found 'em dead. I made up my mind I wouldn't hunt animals no more. It just didn't feel right to kill off anyone's children.

Frank Norfleet - Detective

Oil became big business in Texas. Confidence men came with the wildcatters and sometimes regular folk fell for some scheme or other. When it happened, it was nice to have a real detective as a friend.

PA TOL' ME to get to sleep early so we could leave before dawn. I was excited, so didn't know how I'd get to sleep, but I didn't argue with him none. Pa was takin' me along with him to visit with a friend of his, name of Mr. Norfleet. He owned a big ranch down southeast of us in Hale County.

Mr. Norfleet was an important man in many ways; he was the first foreman of the Spade Ranch, started up his own ranch, raised racehorses, and was a darn good detective. The FBI even gave him a special award for bringin' in all sorts of lawbreakers. His specialty was confidence men, because that's what got him started as a detective.

In 1919, Mr. Norfleet was back east and got taken in by a gang claiming to be mule brokers. He was told he could make good money in the cotton business, but he had to put up a lot of money, near forty-five thousand dollars. Well, he was a successful rancher, so he had that kind of money to invest. The con man and his partners ran off with the money and left Mr. Norfleet high and dry.

He did not take well to bein' gypped, so he went after the men. He followed them all over the country, even into Canada and Mexico. He wore disguises to help him meet up with other bad men to get information. Eventually, he found all of the men; three in California, one in Salt Lake City, and the last two in Georgia. Catchin' those crooks made him famous and a lot of folks started comin' to him for help. He had a reputation of always gettin' his man, just like the Texas Rangers. He even wrote a book about it, Pa said. Pa tol' me the story, but he says never to bring it up to Mr. Norfleet, as it was a raw spot for him.

Pa knew him because Pa was a good horse doctor. He'd gone down to the Norfleet Ranch and helped out when a sickness was takin' the horses. Pa managed to save a few of Mr. Norfleet's racehorses and that not only made Pa some money, but also made the two of them good friends.

Now, Pa needed a favor back. He'd wrote a letter to Mr. Norfleet and was invited to come down to the ranch to lay out the whole story. So, that's how come we were driving over a hundred miles: to get help from one of the best detectives at findin' grifters, swindlers, and all-round no-goods.

When we got to the ranch, we drove right up to the front

of a big two-story house. A wide porch with columns stuck out the front. I ain't seen a house like it except in picture books of what they called plantations. I'll tell you, it was the fanciest house I ever saw, and probably the biggest, too.

A man came right out as soon as we pulled up. First off, I thought it must be one of the Norfleet children, but it turns out it was the man hisself. He was hardly taller than me, but when he got close, his face showed some lines and his head some gray hair.

Pa and he shook hands and patted each other on the back. Both were smilin' pretty big, so it was plain they were glad to see each other.

"Welcome, Louis. I'm surely sorry it took misfortune to get you down this way again."

"Well, Frank, I'm also sorry about not visiting sooner, but a farm keeps a man busy."

"It does that, Louis. Why, I hardly have time to go chasin' after criminals anymore, what with the cattle and the horses." Mr. Norfleet laughed like it was a good joke, and Pa laughed with him.

Pa turned to me and said, "Eddie, say hello to Mr. Norfleet. Frank, this is my boy Edward."

I shook his hand, which gripped mine like he was glad to meet me. He smiled at me and I couldn't help but smile back. He was that kind of man, one who makes everyone welcome, except maybe crooks, that is.

"Edward, if you'd like we'll go out to the barn and you can look over the foals. Then, you can tell me which you think are the winners."

That perked my interest as I did like horses. Pa tol' me Mr. Norfleet started up a whole line of racehorses called the Five Dollar Strain. He named them after a stallion he bought for five dollars and it turned out to not only be a good racehorse, but also his colts bred true to their sire. No small part of Mr. Norfleet's money came from racing horses.

Pa wanted another look at the horses, so we all three headed for the barn. It was just about as fancy as the house, being all whitewashed, but it was even bigger. When we went in, I could see it must have twenty stalls, most of 'em with a horse pokin' his head out over the stall door. In the walkway between the stalls, a groom was brushin' down one of the horses, a sorry lookin' horse if I ever saw one.

"C'mon over, boy, he's gentle enough," the groom said. I walked on up and the horse, who didn't look like much, snuffled at me.

"This is Five Dollar himself," the groom said and handed me a sugar cube. I offered it to the stallion with my palm held flat. He lipped it right off without hardly touchin' my hand at all. Despite him being an ugly horse, I heard he was plenty fast. Mr. Norfleet's five-dollar horse was a real bargain, it turns out.

I looked over the colts and couldn't find anything wrong with 'em. I was hopin' Mr. Norfleet wasn't actually expectin' me to give him advice on his horses. I know cow ponies and mules, but I'd never done much with racin' stock.

While I was lookin' at the horses, Pa and Mr. Norfleet sat down in a couple of chairs by the tack room. I trained one ear their way, but tried not to look like I was eavesdroppin'. They talked about when Pa helped out with the horses, and what they were both up to since then. The groom looked their way, too, then decided it was time to put the stallion back in his stall and go find somethin' else to do.

"I feel sort of stupid, Frank. The man seemed to know what he was talkin' about and I fell for his pitch like some rube."

"No reason to be kickin' yourself, Louis." He chuckled. "After all, I got took for forty-five thousand and you only got took for two hundred. If you say you're a fool, then I've got to be a bigger one."

"You know I don't think that's true. You had a whole squad of con men workin' on you. Besides, you got 'em all in the end."

"That I did, and I'll do my best to catch your con man, too. So, what exactly did this man tell you? First off, did he give you a name and where he was from."

Pa gave him the details, of which I was aware. Pa wasn't the only one to be taken in by the grifter. He was just one of a group putting their money together to buy shares in an oil well. Everybody knew since Spindletop oil was goin' to be big business and it was smart to get in early. My uncle Alex was already pumpin' his own wells over near Tyler. Uncle Alex asked Pa to come over and help, but Pa wanted to stay on the farm, so he thought to invest in oil along with the other farmers.

Well, they soon found out there weren't no oil well and the man took off with all their money. The farmers had no way to know where the man had gone. They'd tol' the Sheriff, of course, but he just shrugged and said if they brought the man in, then he'd arrest him.

Pa figured Mr. Norfleet might be able to find the man as he had what Pa called "connections." I wasn't certain of what that meant, except Mr. Norfleet had ways to catch up to these con men that Pa didn't.

After the situation was laid out, Pa and Mr. Norfleet went on up to the house. They didn't invite me along, so I just stayed out in the barn with the horses. The groom, named Tommy, came out again with another horse and I helped him.

Soon, Pa and Mr. Norfleet came out'n the house and they shook hands and patted backs again. Pa waved me over, we got in the truck, and said our goodbyes.

"What did he say, Pa?" I asked bein' curious if we would get some help.

"Frank – Mr. Norfleet – said not to worry. He made some telephone calls and he thinks he'll have somethin' to tell us in a few days. He's got an old friend, Burke Mathes, checking the state records. Burke's the state representative from Hale County and knows a lot of folks at the Capitol. If anybody can find the cheat, it'd be Burke."

We went on home and nothin' happened for a few days. We just went about our business as usual, not knowin' what to expect.

A couple of weeks later, the Sheriff pulled up to our yard and called Pa out of the barn. I was in the barn, too, so I went along with him.

"Well, Louis, you've had some good luck," the Sheriff said.

"How's that Elmer?"

"I got a call from Burke Mathes last week. You know Burke, right? Anyways, he tol' me to take a drive up to Vega. He says the Sheriff in Oldham County had a little surprise for me."

"That's interestin', Elmer, but what's it got to do with me?" Pa asked.

"He was holdin' the confidence man who took your money. "

"That is good news."

"Seems like he'd tried the same thing up there, but Burke Mathes already clued them to be on the lookout. Burke, he'd called every Sheriff in the whole panhandle to tell 'em the same thing."

"Did the man have our money?"

"Sorry to say, he didn't have all the money, but still had some left. He confessed once the Sheriff took him in. Gave his name as Samuel Clemens."

"Samuel Clemens, you say? He tol' me his name was John Donne." Pa looked a little puzzled, then said, "You all might want to check a little more on the name."

"Why? He gave himself up easy enough and told his name right off."

"Well," Pa said , "Samuel Clemens is the real name of Mark Twain, the writer."

"Oh. Why I knew that. I just assumed it was a coincidence."

I thought the Sheriff was gettin' a little red around his collar. I had to put my hand over my face so's he wouldn't see my smile. I'd been readin' ol' Mark Twain's books for years now, so I knew his real name. I didn't think the Sheriff did, though.

Still, he did bring good news. The Circuit Judge was callin' a meetin' of the people who'd lost money, so he could make sure everybody got what portion they were due. Pa wouldn't get back all his money, but as he said later, he'd paid his ticket for bein' taken in.

I asked Pa why he hadn't just called the counties round about and accomplish the same thing Mr. Norfleet and Mr. Mathes had done.

Pa said, "Edward, I tend horses and grow crops. I'm real good at it, but I don't have what those two men have--the experience in dealin' with lawbreakers. Now, Frank got into detective work because somebody did him wrong. It worked fine for him, but I couldn't have done what he did. The folks voted for Burke so's he'd take care of things for them."

"I think I might be interested in bein' a detective someday, or maybe I could join the Texas Rangers."

Pa laughed, but not like he was makin' fun of me. He never did make fun of me. "I always say, Edward, do what you do best and hire out the rest."

I thought it was good advice from Pa, but he always was comin' up with good advice for me. Now, if I could just remember it all, I'd be in fine shape.

The Cattle Drive

You can't talk about Texas without mentioning cattle. Just about every little boy wanted to grow up to be a cowboy, although it was an occupation few would ever take up. For one brief and shining moment, Eddie realized his dream of being a real cowboy.

I SEEN the dust cloud down the road, so naturally I jumped up to the top rail of the fence to get a better look. It took about ten minutes before I could make out a couple of drovers was pushin' a small herd up the road. By then, Pa come over to find out why I wasn't doin' my chores. The two of us were standin' on the fence rail, peerin' down the road. Ma came out of the house, but she stayed up on the porch with her hand shadin' her eyes.

When we saw it was a herd, Pa shook his head and grinned.

"I ain't seen that for some years," he said.

Well, what could we do but wait for the drovers to come on up to the gate? After all, we was the only place close by and knew these fellas would need some water, at the least, and maybe a meal to go with it.

Ma went back in the house and when I saw the little puff of smoke from the chimney, I knew she was already firin' up the stove. The angle of the sun over the barn told me it was 'bout four. It was close enough to suppertime I hoped the herd would have to stop for the night.

With us bein' fifteen miles from town and six miles by road to the nearest neighbor, I'd be pretty excited we were gettin' any kind of visitors, but a cattle herd, that was almost too much to ask for.

I jumped off the fence like a lightnin' bolt and headed for the corral. Old Sam was closest so I grabbed a rope and threw it round his neck for reins. Sam's really easy, so I didn't bother with a bridle and ridin' bareback is second nature to me. It took a little shufflin' to convince Sam to sidle over by the fence so I could get on. After all, he's near sixteen hands and I'm not very tall. Pa saw what I was doin' and nodded to me. I was gonna ask before I lit out, but he beat me to it.

Sam and me trotted down the road. I was bouncin' and grinnin' so hard my teeth kept clackin' together. We met the front of the herd a quarter mile later and my jaw just near dropped off my face. I couldn't believe what I was seein' so I shut my mouth again and looked really hard.

Yep, I'm here to tell ya and ya know I don't lie. Every last animal in the herd was a bull. This puzzled me no end, as much as it puzzles you to hear it. Course, the herd was no more 'n twenty Hereford bulls, but . . .well, I can't think of what that would be. Mostly herds are made up of steers and cows. Bulls ain't usually included as they cause troubles wantin' at the cows and all.

One of the drovers pulled off and stood waitin' for me when I trotted up on Sam.

"Howdy," he saaid and I howdied him back. He pulled his hat off and squinted up the road to our place. "Your place?" he asked. I answered him, "Yessir," like I was taught and waited for him to make the next move.

"Think your Pa could spare some water?"

"Yessir. He just tol' me to come tell you just that thing. Ma's heatin' up the stove too, if you'd like some supper."

"That's mighty nice, son. What do they call you?"

"Edward," I said so I'd sound older than someone called Eddie.

"Well, Edward, let's move these bulls on up the road."

So, I just pulled Sam up to the side of the herd and whooped a couple of times to keep 'em movin'. This was the best, I thought. I'd only got to read about the cowboys and now I got to be one, at least for a few minutes.

So, on we went, keepin' those bulls in line. If the truth be known, they didn't need any encouragin'. They smelled the water and didn't need invitin' to keep movin'.

West Texas in the summer is just about as hot and dry a place as the world's got to offer. I'd seen a picture show about the Sahara Desert and I think it might be just a little hotter and a little drier, but not much. I didn't know exactly where these drovers come from, but I knew my neighborhood and the nearest supply of good water is in the exact opposite direction. I figured those bulls were mighty thirsty no matter which way they come.

Pa opened the corral gate and shooed out the horses by the time we pulled in. The bulls headed right on into the corral with no fuss. I could see over to the other side Sister was pumpin' for all she was worth to fill the trough as the bulls crowded up for a drink.

We closed up the gate and I jumped off Sam and let him go find his friends. I could see the other horses were already makin' a beeline for the barn. They liked the shade and the hay that's always in the stalls. Pa doesn't let the horses stay in the barn all day, though, so they were just as happy to get in out of the sun.

Pa and the man were talkin' by now so I went back over to listen. They just sort of chatted, like grownups do, about weather and crops and such. I started gettin' antsy listenin' to all this. Why not cut right to it and ask? Why were they pushin' a herd of bulls and where were they takin' 'em?

Finally, the man says "Me and Mike over there are takin' these bulls to Clovis. From there, they're goin' to the Spade Ranch. They're needin' some new blood in their herds. I believe they're tryin' to cross 'em with the long horns. No matter to me, I'm just takin' 'em over.

Pa considered this for a while. Seems like every time one of 'em says somethin', the other one's gotta think it over for five minutes 'fore they answer. This made me a little crazy and I started to rock back and forth from one foot to another. Pa shifted a look my way, which I know exactly what it means. I tryed hard to stand still.

"That's most forty, fifty miles from here," Pa said.

"Yeah, it's quite aways to herd bulls," the man agreed, "but I've already pushed 'em fifty miles with just the two of us."

"Why didn't you truck 'em?" Pa asked reasonably.

"I thought about it, but it'd cost more'n I've got to spend. If they walk, I can take them cross-country. It saves me quite a bit." He stood thinkin' awhile, then said, "I decided it was the best route to take them over to Clovis and put them on the train to Anton. Two train rides cuts my profit too much."

"Well, I can appreciate it," Pa replied. I was just a kid, but even I knew 1931 ain't a very good year for West Texas ranchers and farmers. Pa said the whole country's goin' bad.

Pa went on to invite the man and his hand to supper and the offer was accepted with thanks.

The man's name was Jed Browning. The bulls don't all belong to him. He'd made the deal with the broker and he'd collected all the bulls folks had to spare from around his place up west of Amarillo. He lived about forty miles from us, so we didn't know him, of course.

Seems like these bulls were all Herefords and come from a

really important bull some man imported all the way from a town called Hereford in England. I guess that's how they named the town where they come from. Probably it was how they named our closest town, too. Herefords from Hereford goin' through Hereford, Texas. I thought it was passably funny right there.

Now all of that weren't important to me. When Pa and Mr. Browning headed into the house, I climbed up on the corral fence and just looked at those bulls. I can tell you straight up, I want to be a rancher, not a farmer, so those bulls looked awfully good to me.

They were road-dirty and their heads hung down in the heat, but to me they were just about as beautiful as can be. Here, I lived in Texas and we didn't even own any cattle ?cepting an old milk cow. I didn't think it was fair. I wanted to rope and brand cattle and ride the range and, instead, I got to do chores on a pig farm. Well, almost a pig farm. That's the most livestock we had, other than the mules and horses. Pa planted row crops and wheat on six hundred forty acres, but it wasn't doin' too good. Seemed like it was hotter and drier this year.

Ended up Mr. Browning and Mike stayed the night with the bulls milling around in our pen. That evenin', Pa and Mr. Browning discussed the drive ?cross to Clovis and I'm listenin' really close. Finally, Mr. Browning eyed me sittin' there and stopped to think a minute. He turned to Pa and said, "I sure could use some help with this herd. Would you consider lettin' Edward here come along to help?"

My ears perked up like I was a hound dog gettin' scent on a raccoon. Pa considered a bit and then to my surprise he said yes. I was going on a real cattle drive!

I was so excited I could hardly sleep that night and I was up and ready to go at dawn. I even had Sam saddled up. Pa mentioned he thought Sam was the steadiest and knew cattle, so I should take him and not my own horse, Brownie. I was a tad disappointed since Sam was, well, what can I say, Sam was somethin' of an ol' plug. But, I wasn't complainin'. No sirree.

I waved to Ma standin' on the porch. She hollered, "you mind Mr. Browning or I'll tan you good." This was just her way of sayin' goodbye. Pa shook my hand and slapped Sam on the hindquarters to get him moving. That made me feel like I was all grown up.

We brought the bulls out of the pen, got them headed in the right direction then set off for the long ride to Clovis.

We were off. Goin' on a real drive and I'd be gone overnight for the first time in my life. Matter of fact, I'd be away from home for near eight days with five days herdin' the bulls to Clovis then two and a half me comin' back. Mr. Browning told Pa once we got the bulls to Clovis, I'd be paid one dollar and fifty cents and I'd come back home on my own. Me, I woulda done it for free.

I felt like I was a real cowboy. I took out my lariat and swung it next to the bull's head when one tried to wander out of line. I yipped and hollered and generally acted like I thought a cowboy ought to be.

We hadn't gone but a few miles when Mr. Browning trotted on over to my position and rode next to me.

He said, "You know these parts, son?"

I replied, "I know 'em as well as anyone round here, I s'pect."

"Well," he said, "maybe you can direct us to some watering hole hereabouts?"

So, that's why Mr. Browning wanted me to come along. It wasn't for me bein' good at herdin' cattle since I hadn't herded any cattle before, except our old milk cow. I felt a mite prideful 'cause even if I was only eleven, almost, I did know these parts real well. Me and Sister, had been all over the place within twenty miles of our farm. Heck, we rode to school every day and it was more'n six miles from home.

I allowed to him if we veered off a bit to the southwest, there was a playa that held water until late in the spring. Since it was early June, I suspected it would still have some.

I pointed a bit southwest from where we were headin'. Mr. Browning nodded to me then booted his horse on over to his hired hand, Mike, pointin' off the way we'd be goin'. We started to turn the bulls a little at a time until we were headin' in the right direction.

I hadn't mentioned much about the hired hand, but maybe I should speak on him now. Mr. Browning introduced the man as just Mike and didn't add much else. I don't think Mike said two words at our ranch, and I didn't speak to him myself. Mostly, I didn't feel good about calling a growed man by just his first name. Pa would box my ears if I did that. So, I wondered about him and started callin' him Mr. Mike in my head since otherwise didn't feel right.

He was quiet, like I said, and wore a beard, but not like it was meant to be a full beard, but just like he hadn't had a chance to shave for a week. Mr. Browning was clean shaved, so I knew it wasn't ?cause he didn't have the chance. Also, his clothes weren't really right for what we was doin'. His boots weren't cowboy style, but lace ups like soldiers wore. He had on a jacket over a plain shirt, but neither one was what I'd think of a cowboy wearin'.

I suspected he weren't really a cowboy at all, but he seemed to ride good enough to be a help. He did cut off the bulls when they wanted to head somewhere else and generally kept them movin' where they ought to go. It was gettin' so men were losin' their regular jobs and turned to doin' anything handy to put bread on the table.

When we reached the playa, I told Mr. Browning about, we stopped to let the bulls and horses drink. The water was a little low and the banks muddy, but it did have enough for the animals. Mr. Browning allowed it was a good time to break for a meal and a rest. The animals needed to graze awhile and, it still bein' spring, there was a good layer of buffalo grass on the prairie.

We went on like this for four more days. Start up the herd in the mornin', find water, stop around noon for some food, and tuck in for the night at sundown. I'll have to admit even I was getting a little saddle-sore by the time we reached Clovis.

We took those bulls right down the main street. People stopped and stared as we moved 'em along. The bulls were pretty tuckered out by then, so they didn't even care. I sat up straighter in the saddle and swung my rope a few times just for show. Those bulls weren't headin' anywhere but straight down the street.

At the end of the street was the train yard. Since Clovis was still pretty much in cattle country, the yard was mostly made up of lots of small corrals where cattle milled and lowed. It was right noisy down here. We was met by the yard crew. I don't think they knew we was comin' but they jumped right in and turned the bulls into one of the holdin' pens. My job was done.

Mr. Browning spent some time shoutin' orders to the yard crew and when everything was settled, he came over where I was standin' by Sam. I'd got off and loosed up the cinch so he could relax for a bit.

"Thanks, Edward, you did a real good job," he said smilin' at me. Then, he reached into his wallet and hauled out two dollars bills.

"I ain't got change, Mr. Browning," I said real polite like Ma taught me.

"That's okay, Edward. I reckon you earned a little extra." I grinned real big cause two dollars was a lot of money for me. I shook his hand and waved goodbye to Mike, though he still didn't say a word.

I tightened up Sam's cinch and swung on up. First thing, I'd need to find a store so I could get somethin' to eat for the way back home. It was easy enough since Clovis was pretty much only the train yard and the main street. I got some bread and a couple cans of beans for the trip. It cost me twenty-five cents, so I still had plenty left for some candy. Since it was only about noon, I decided to start back right away. No sense in wastin' daylight, I figured.

It didn't take long to get out of New Mexico and back into Texas. I'll have to say I felt easier once I was back. I don't know about those New Mexico folks, but I knew I'd be fine in Texas 'cause Texas was my home.

I kept an eye peeled for the green grass showing where water was still on the ground and found a nice place to camp for the night. The playa lay out by an old windmill that creaked when the wind turned the arms. No sign of a house or corrals or anything looking like people ever lived near by, so I just settled in by the windmill for the night. Bread and beans filled my belly well enough. I hobbled Sam so he could graze, but not get too far away.

I sat there by the windmill with a little fire to heat up my beans and looked up at the sky thinkin' about how lucky I was to be a cowboy.

One Fine Dog

Dogs weren't just pets, but working members of the family. Sometimes, they could do amazing things and perform feats that were almost like magic.

MA YELLED LOUD enough for me to hear into the next state. "Edward Preston! Get yerself in here right now!"

I wondered what it was I done now. I didn't recall any particular mischief I'd been up to. At least, not today. I finished throwin' the hay into Beau's corral and went on the run up to the house.

"Yes'm," I said soon as I got to the porch where Ma was standin' with her fists planted on her hips. I reckon you know the look she was givin' me. If'n your mother called you by your first and middle names, then you know exactly what I'm talkin' about.

Then, she surprised me 'cause she smiled. Now, that sure weren't the normal expression she'd have if she was about to give me what-for. I thought maybe she was just havin' some fun with me.

"Your Pa is goin' to pick up the ewes from the Braddock's

place, so go help him get the truck out of the barn."

I grinned myself and almost shouted "Yes'm!" But, I caught myself in time as Ma doesn't like us to be yellin'. I took off to the barn to find Pa. He was already pullin' the tarp off the truck, so I went about helpin' him finish up. We got behind the truck and pushed 'er out of the barn. I jumped in behind the wheel. Like Pa taught me, I checked to make sure the hand brake was on, then I checked the spark and gas levers on the steering column. I pulled up on the spark and pushed down on the gas. Pa gave a mighty pull up on the crank. When the engine roared, I pushed the gas lever up a little more.

"You gotta give it more gas a little faster, Eddie." Pa was tryin' to teach me how to operate the truck as I was goin' on eleven, which is plenty old enough to drive. He was takin' it slower than I'd like. I thought I had the basics down already. Brake. Spark. Throttle. Crank. Throttle. Take off the brake and go!

"Yessir, Pa."

Then, I got my second surprise of the day when Pa went to the passenger side and got in. Now my grin was gettin' even wider, but I tried to tuck it down and act grownup. Pa was goin' to let me drive!

I drove out to the road half expectin' Pa to only let me take the truck that far, but he waves me ahead and we turn left toward the Braddock's.

I should explain what we were doin'. We have some ewes, but we don't have a ram. So, in the fall, we bring the ewes to the Braddocks, who do have a ram. We'd just let them winter over with the Braddock flock. Now, it was spring and the *hijadores*, who came round to help with the lambing, had finished their work. It was time to put the ewes back into our own pastures.

It was only a couple of miles down the road, so I drove slow enough to please Pa and to make my first time at the wheel last a mite longer. At the gate into the sheep field, Pa jumped out and pulled the gate open. I drove on through and up to the sheep pens out by the old windmill. Pa closed up the gate, so the sheep wouldn't make a break fer it.

Mr. Braddock musta known we were comin' as he was waitin for us. I drove the truck up, but knew I wasn't good enough to back it up to the loading chute. The sheep weren't in the pen, so I knew we'd have to go round 'em up. Mr. Braddock owned a sheepdog name of Pete, so it wouldn't be too hard.

Pa and Mr. Braddock commenced talkin', which grown men always spend a long time doin' every time they meet up. One day, I'd have to listen in and see what they found to talk about. After all, I was gettin' to the age I might be expected to carry on these conversations. But, for now, it wasn't my job.

I looked across the big field at the sheep clear to the other side. It was a pretty picture with the new grass so green and the sheep lookin' like a cloud against the blue sky. Mr. Braddock's flock ran about a hundred sheep. Pa tol' me back in the last century there were millions of sheep in West Texas. Mexicans, called *pastores*, followed these sheep in a grazin' route along the Canadian River. But, when the cattle ranchers started buildin' up the big herds, they didn't want the sheep eatin' up all the grass. Back in the 1880s, the Sheep Wars eventually chased off the *pastores*, and cattlemen took over just about all the good land after that.

Now, there weren't too many sheep around. A few lone sheepherders still moved flocks, but none of them very big. We kept just a few sheep for mutton and wool. Ma still carded wool even though you could buy yarn in the stores. I think she liked it better when she did it herself.

It was about a quarter mile across the pasture, so we'd have to walk on over to get them movin'. Pete, Mr. Braddock's dog, would do most of the work, but even a real good sheepdog couldn't move the whole flock all by hisself. And, we'd need to cut our own outta the flock.

First, we'd have to figure out which were our ewes. We'd docked their ears with our mark, but you had to get close enough to read it. Since the ewes were skittish right after lambing, jest like moms everywhere, they worried about their young'uns. We were countin' on motherly love to help us match the lambs belonging to our ewes.

Finally, Pa and Mr. Braddock were done talkin', so we commenced to walk across the pasture. Pete knew what was up so he took off runnin' toward the flock. The ground was still spongy with the spring rains, so it was hard goin' for us. We squished along as best we could. I began to get the idea this wasn't goin' to be so easy after all.

Pete was near the flock by now and he started barkin' up a storm.

"What's got into him? He knows better'n that," Mr. Braddock said with a puzzled look.

Then I saw what was gettin' Pete so riled up. I pointed up and Pa's and Mr. Braddock's eyes followed where I was pointin'. A big golden eagle was soarin' above the herd. He was circling round so it was clear he was lookin' to take a lamb. The sheep got wind of him and started to get excited.

A flock of sheep on the move is like a school of fish. The front ewe turns one way and the whole bunch of them turn with her just like they were readin' her mind. It's quite a sight to behold. First they swarmed one way, then Pete came up to the flank and turned them the other. They were weavin' back and forth across the field with Pete doin' his durndest to head them toward the pens. We were helpin' as much as we could with our boots stuck in the mud as they were.

Suddenly, the eagle nosed down and dove right for the sheep. He disappeared in the middle of 'em, but you could see where he'd gone 'cause the sheep at that spot were not only runnin', but now they started jumpin'. So, if you can picture this, there's this big wave of wooly sheep zigzaggin' across the field with the middle of the flock eruptin' like a wooly geyser. I didn't know they could jump that high. I started to runnin' for the flock to see if'n I could chase off the eagle, but the durned muddy ground tripped me up. I felt flat on my face after only a couple of steps. All I could do is watch.

The eagle took off again and he held a lamb in his claws. This near gave Pete a fit. After all, this was his bunch of sheep and no eagle was goin' to take even one! Pete leaped up on the backs of the flock and jumped from sheep to sheep to get to the middle. The eagle was strugglin' to hold on to the lamb, but hadn't got much altitude; it was more than he could carry off easy. When Pete reached the middle of the sheep geyser, he jumped up himself and grabbed the lamb's leg. Well, that was just too much for the eagle, so he let go of the lamb and took off.

Pete and the lamb came down and disappeared in the sheep wave. We just watched as there wasn't a thing we could do.

The sheep started to slow down since the eagle was gone and pretty soon, Pete popped up in the middle of the flock and jumped out just like he'd jumped in.

"I ain't never seen anything like that before," Pa said, shakin' his head.

"Oh, Pete does that all the time. He knows the quickest way from one side of the flock to t'other is a straight line."

"That's one fine dog, John," my Pa said, still lookin' somewhat amazed.

"Yep. One fine dog," was all Mr. Braddock said, but he was grinnin' from ear to ear. I was thinkin' he could hardly wait to tell the story to the neighbors.

We finally rounded up our sheep and got 'em loaded in the back of the truck. We found the lamb and saw he was fine except for a little scratch on the leg where Pete grabbed hold. I was thinkin' I could hardly wait for school the next day as I'd get some pleasure from tellin' the story, too.

Mr. Young's Arkansas Cedar Float

All work and no play is not a way to grow up properly. Going fishing was an easy and cheap way to do both at the same time—catch some fish for dinner while enjoying a lazy afternoon by the creek.

EVER' ONCE IN awhile, Pa lets me take off from my chores to go fishin'. This was one of those days, so I asked Ma if she could pack up some food to take along. She was agreeable to it, and made me a good meal with sandwiches and even a piece of chocolate cake. I filled my canteen at the pump.

I went out to the corral and chased Brownie a couple of times around the corral 'til I caught up with him in a corner. He was a darn good horse once you managed to get a rope on him, but he sure did like to make you work for it. I saddled him up and threw the saddlebags with my lunch over the back of the saddle. I slid my fishing' pole into the rifle scabbard. It stuck out a ways, but was easier than carrying it all the way in my hands.

It was about eight miles to the creek with the best fishin', but I needed to stop at the Young's place for a fishin' float. Mr. Young made the floats hisself out of Arkansas cedar. He considered them to be the best floats and I won't dispute the claim as they'd worked for me in the past.

When I got to their place, Mr. Young was out in the barn, so I just rode up there straightaway.

Howdy, Mr. Young," I said, "I'd sure appreciate borrowin' one of your fine floats."

"You sure can, Eddie," he replied right off. He went over to a cupboard he'd nailed up in the barn. I got down off Brownie and walked on over. The cupboard was full of fishin' gear, but mostly it held floats, dozens of 'em, in all sizes. We discussed what I was goin' for, which happened to be perch, and he looked over my pole before choosin' one for me.

"Now, you be real careful with this, Eddie. I've told you before these floats are made of Arkansas cedar and it ain't easy gettin' that wood."

"I sure will, Mr. Young, and I surely do appreciate the loan."

I put the float into my saddlebag and mounted up. I headed down the road and waved goodbye to him and he waved back. I was all set and ready to catch some fish.

It took over'n hour to reach the creek, but I'd left early enough I had all afternoon to fish. I took all the gear off Brownie and put some hobbles on him so he wouldn't go home without me. I settled in by the creek and tied the float to the line. I cast out away and then stuck the pole into a crack in some rocks while I ate my lunch. Bees were buzzin' and the birds chirpin'. It was just a downright nice day. I'm afraid I kind of dozed off once. A fish got on my line and pulled my pole right out of the crack while I was snoozin'. I needed to wade out to get hold of it again. Other'n that, I had no problems and managed to catch a few fish, which I cleaned right away to keep 'em fresh.

It was time to go around about three o'clock. I packed everything up and headed back. I was goin' along pretty good as Brownie saw we were goin' home. He usually moved a mite faster on a comin' back than a goin' to.

I'd got about half way home, when I realized I didn't put the float back in my saddlebag. I stopped and checked. Sure enough, I'd left that danged float back at the creek. I turned Brownie around, which he didn't like at all, and headed for the creek again.

I found the float easy enough. It was sittin' right where I'd been fishin'. Now, it was really gettin' late, so I kicked up Brownie to a fast trot goin' back to the Young's place.

We got there and Mr. Young was still out in the barn. He did spend a goodly amount of time out there. Anyways, I got off Brownie and dug the float out'n my saddlebags.

"Thanks for the loan, Mr. Young," I says like Ma taught me.

"Oh, that's okay Eddie. You can just keep it. I got plenty of 'em," he says.

I thought how it would have been easier if'n he'd just give me the float in the first place. But, it was the way things were, so I just thanked him and started out toward home. I was glad to have the float. Too bad I had to dump the fish I'd caught. They'd just been out of the creek too long.

By this time, it was gettin' near sunset. Now, I'm not afeared of the dark, but I didn't like to ride when it was pitch black neither. It was gettin' darker all the time, and I still had a couple of miles to go when I saw a campfire on the hillside, not far off the road.

I thought about it awhile, and decided to stop at the camp and see who was there. It might be a neighbor camped out for some reason. Certain times of the year, like when the cows are calvin', any number of people might be camped out on the prairie.

When I reached the campfire, a dog came up to greet me. I saw he was a sheepdog, so I figured the camp belonged to one of the herders what kept their flocks around these parts. I saw a little chuck wagon, too. It was hardly six feet long and just wide enough to hold a single driver. A man was crouched down by the campfire and workin' away with a big iron skillet.

"Howdy," I said, and the man looked up. I could see he was Mexican and thought maybe he didn't speak English as he didn't answer me right away. He just looked at me kind of sharp like he was sizin' me up. Finally, he stood up and waved me over to the campfire. I got down off Brownie and walked over.

The smell hit me like a rock fell on my head. I never smelled anything so good in all my life. I knew right away this man could really handle camp cookin'. First, I got a waft of sourdough—biscuits, I figured. Then, the smell of the mutton stew came over me and my stomach started jerkin' and grumblin'. It'd been quite awhile since Ma's lunch and I was pretty hungry.

"*Sientese por favor,*" he said and I knew for sure he was Mexican. "*¿Le gustaria un poco de guisado de cordero?*" He pointed at the skillet.

I figured out he was asking me to stay for dinner. "*Si, me encantaria. Gracias Señor,*" I answered, hopin' my little bit of Spanish was close to right.

He heaped up a big plate of stew and sourdough biscuits for me. We sat there by the campfire, neither one of us sayin' a word. I guess he could tell by how I pronounced the Spanish I wasn't very good at it. Since he didn't offer to speak in English, I assumed it wasn't a language he knew very well either.

I've got to tell you, that sheepherder made sourdough biscuits even better than Ma's. I wouldn't tell her, but it's the truth. Maybe it was I was so hungry or maybe it was we were sittin' out on the prairie under the stars, but whatever it was, I hardly ever enjoyed a meal so much as that one.

When I was finished, the man took my plate and handed it over to the dog to lick clean, not that I left much there. I nodded to him and said, "*gracias.*" I rubbed my stomach, too, so he'd know I liked the food.

He said, "*de nada*," and went about cleanin' up.

"I've got to go home now," I said, not knowin' the Spanish, but he nodded like he knew what I was sayin'.

I walked over to Brownie where he was ground-tied and got into my saddlebags. I took out the float and brought it over to the man. First, he shook his head and waved me off. "No, no." I set the float down by the campfire.

"*Gracias*," I said again and got up on Brownie.

We went on home and I'll have to say Ma was none too pleased by me gettin' back so late, but she forgave me, like she always does. Later, I told Pa about the meal with the sheepherder and givin' him the float.

He looked at me for awhile, then said, "Eddie, you gotta learn more Spanish if you're goin' to live in Texas."

I figured Pa was right. He most always was.

Beau the Jack

After Pa bought the jackass at the auction, Bucephalus earned his keep as a stud. However, he did provide some excitement on occasion.

A LOT OF people think a Jackass is just a mule. They'd be only half right since a Jackass is the daddy to a mule, with the mama bein' a mare. You might hear someone call somebody else "son of a jack." Well, that's just polite language for sayin' they're a mule.

Now, in the south, a Jack is a valuable animal. They give the mule the brawn and the brains they're famous for. One line of jackasses is called a Mammoth Jack. It can be up to eighteen hands high at the withers. For you city folk, that's six feet to the base of the neck.

Pa named our Mammoth Jack Bucephalus, after Alexander the Great's horse. I'm not sure why, except Pa liked ancient history and I think the name appealed to him.

Beau, as we took to callin' him, was about as big as a Jack can get and every inch of him as mean as can be. When I'd go out to throw him some hay, I stood back a few feet 'cause he'd snake his old head over the fence and clamp down with his big teeth wherever he could grab on. I'd got more'n one bruise 'til I learned to stay way back. Course, a lot of hay got throwed on the ground, but I figured it was just too bad for Beau.

What I most dreaded, though, was when we took Beau out for breedin'. He was a pretty popular stud around here cause he was so big. The ranchers and farmers brought their mares to our place for the meet-up. We'd take the mares in to the barn and put them in a special stall so narrow so they couldn't turn around. At the back, the business end my Pa calls it, a short gate would keep the mares from kickin' but allowed Beau room to work.

The bad part was trying to catch Beau and bring him to the barn. Not that he wasn't willin', mind you, he was just in more of a hurry than we were. Pa always handled Beau 'cause I was too small to hold onto him. But, I was expected to help out by openin' the gates and closin' 'em behind. That took some runnin' as Beau would be movin' pretty fast just as soon as Pa buckled the halter on him. Once he didn't even wait for me to open up the gate. Later, we replaced the wood gate with a metal one. Jacks are pretty smart and once he knew he could go through the gate, he'd not wait to do it again. His corral was made of eight-inch posts with one by twelve planks, so you can guess it was pretty strong.

The mares came into season in the spring, so that's when Beau was busiest. Pa decided to make the fetchin' a mite easier by keepin' Beau's halter with a lead rope on him. The six foot lead slowed Beau down some, but mostly it didn't bother him to have it on all the time.

We found out right soon this wasn't a good idea. One mornin' we'd come out to greet another farmer with his mare and we went round to the corral to fetch Beau. First off we didn't see him and we thought he'd got himself out in the middle of the night. When we got closer, though, we saw he was lyin' on his side near the fence, but he holdin' his head way too high to be natural.

We took out runnin' and come to see Beau got that six-foot lead wrapped around his neck and he was stranglin' hisself on the fence. He was up too close to the fence to get his feet under him, so all's he could do is hold his head as high as he could. We could hear him gaspin' for air.

Pa jumped right over the fence. I was mighty surprised 'cause I didn't think he was that spry. But he was, and he started pullin' on the rope tryin' to get it from around Beau's neck. Of course, Beau was not cooperatin' so he was kickin' and thrashin'. I was worried Pa would be kicked.

The farmer quick handed Pa his foldin' knife with the blade out, but Pa seed it ain't too sharp. Pa yelled at me, "Eddie, go get a big knife from your Ma!" Course, I took out like my pants're on fire and ran up to the house.

"Ma, Ma," I screamed, "gimme a knife, gimme a knife!" Well, Ma don't just hand over knives to eight-year-olds, so she grabbed my arm and gave me a shake to settle me down.

"Eddie, you settle down. Now, what you want with a knife?" she asked. A reasonable question, but I don't have breath to give her a reasonable answer.

I just pointed, sort of jumpin' up and down and the same time and yelled "Beau's a chokin'!"

Ma's a pretty smart woman, so that's all it took and she handed me the biggest butcher knife she had. I took out as fast as I could and she's yellin' after me, "Point it to the ground! Sakes alive, boy, you'll fall and cut yerself!"

I pointed the knife down to the ground and kept runnin' til I got back to the corral. Pa's still wrestlin' with Beau, who's really bad off now. I didn't think he was breathin' and I could see his eyes all rolled up and only the whites showin'.

I slid the knife through the fence and Pa started sawin' on the rope as hard as he can. I'm worried 'cause I see Pa's bleedin' from a cut on his face. I thought maybe he should just let Beau choke to death.

Soon enough, Pa'd cut through the rope and Beau heaved himself up on all fours and stood head down, finally breathin' again. We all just stood there watchin' to see if Beau was goin' to stay on his feet or not.

After a couple of minutes, Beau staggered off to the other side of the corral and Pa handed me the knife through the fence. He walked over to the gate rather than comin' back over the fence again. He was lookin' a mite worse for wear, too.

Pa told the farmer to leave his mare up in the barn, but we'd not be takin' Beau out of the corral today.

The next mornin' we went out to collect Beau for the mare. Instead of pullin' and fightin', he was standin' just like a gentleman. He followed Pa out of the corral as quiet as he could be. After that day, old Beau was gentle as a lamb. I'm thinkin' his brain might've got messed up when he couldn't breathe, but Pa says Beau just learned his lesson. I'm not sure one way or t'other myself, but I was just happy he wasn't tryin' to bite me anymore.

No Angel

Idle hands are the devil's workshop. So goes an old saying. A boy with nothing much to do can sometimes find the worst possible things to do.

FROM WHAT YOU'VE heard about me, you might come to the conclusion I was a well-behaved child. Well, I don't mean to give you a false picture of what I'm really like. I know it's hard to believe, but sometimes I did stuff that was not exactly admired by my Ma and Pa. I wasn't exactly the devil, but I weren't no angel neither.

Ma and Pa liked to go to town, that bein' Hereford, on Saturday nights. They'd visit friends and sometimes eat at the diner. They left me home to take care of Sister, which is what we call my sister Dorothy. Generally, we behaved ourselves as we knew the consequences if we didn't. One of them Saturdays, I was outside not doin' much of anything. You know, just watchin' the clouds and throwin' rocks and so on.

I noticed a flock of blackbirds lit on Ma's clothesline, so I went in and got the shotgun. I loaded it with smallshot and snuck around the side of the house so's not to scare the birds. I figured I could get the whole flock of birds if I shot straight down the clothesline from one end to the other.

I had to be real quiet, so's I thought I'd sneak up on 'em like I was a Comanche. I got down on my belly and rested the shotgun across my arms. The grass was high enough so I'd not be seen. I dug in my elbows and pulled myself real slow around the corner of the house. When I got to the lilac bush, I got up behind it and checked if the birds had a notion I was there. They just sat on the line and didn't even look my way, so I hunched over and ran lickety-split to the oak tree. From there, I was right at the end of the line and no more'n ten feet away. I leaned around the tree trunk and eyed the line. Yep, I could see right down it. My hands aren't big enough to span both triggers, so I had to pull them one at a time. I figured I'd shoot the first barrel and then real quick-like, fire off the second. That way, I'd get to hit the flock twice.

I eased the shotgun up to my shoulder and pulled back slow on the left-hand trigger. The first shot blasted off and knocked me back a few feet where I landed on my rear-end real hard. I still held the shotgun in my hands, but I wasn't in any position to fire off the second barrel. When I sat up and looked to see how many birds I got, I was in for a shock. All that noise and not one feather to show for it. But Ma's clothesline...now that's a different story. The durn thing looked like a dead snake layin' there.

I knew right away Ma would not be pleased with this.

I got myself up and was wonderin' what to do next when I looked up and saw the blackbirds flyin' in a circle like they were waitin' for the clothesline to be put back up for 'em to light on.

Well, that burned me up they were so cheeky. To get even with 'em, I set the butt of the shotgun on the ground, pointed it up at those birds and, standin' to the side, pulled the second trigger. Boom! The birds flew up in the air, but I got me a little flashburn on my face from the waddin'. I hadn't leaned far enough away, I guess.

My ears was ringin', but I decided I'd better get some twine and string a new clothesline before Ma got home. When I started up to the house, I saw Sister standin' on the porch, laughin' her fool head off. Of course, she'd watched the whole darn thing. Now, I knew if I were goin' to get away without a whippin', I'd have to come to an understandin' with her.

"Sister," I called out in a real sweet voice.

She took one look at the gun in my hands, shrieked and ran into the house, slammin' the door behind her. By the time I reached the porch, she'd thrown the bolt and locked me out.

"C'mon now. I ain't gonna hurt you."

I could hear her laughin' behind the door. That peeved me even more. "I just need to get some twine so's I can fix the clothesline. You unlock the door and let me in," I said as nice as you please.

"No way, Eddie, you'll beat me up to make me be quiet."

"Now, why would I do that? Sure, I don't want you to tell Ma, but there ain't no reason for me to beat you up."

She seemed to think about this for awhile, then she finally

unlatched the door. I jumped through before she could change her mind.

I grabbed her by one pigtail as she was tryin' to hightail it to the kitchen.

"I won't beat you up now, but if'n you tell Ma, I'll whip you good," I said, mean like, so she'd know I was serious.

She started cryin' so I let go of her hair.

"You promise me," I yelled at her. I knew bein' mean only went so far with Sister.

"Oh, quit bawlin', you little baby. Just shut your mouth and I won't beat you up."

She snuffled a little more, but seemed to be done with the cryin'. I felt bad about yellin' at her, but this was serious business. If Ma found out about the clothesline, then I'd be marched to the woodshed.

So, I went to the loft and got out the box I kept hid under the bed. I shuffled through and found some jawbreakers.

I gave the jawbreakers to Sister and got her to promise not to tell. I hoped she'd remember her promise. If she tol' then I'd have no choice but to follow up on my threat. If you don't keep your promises, nobody will believe you next time.

I found some twine and went back out to put up a new clothesline. I dragged the ladder from the barn along with the hammer and some nails. I was almost done when I saw the cloud of dust on the road signaling Ma and Pa were on their way. I hurried up and drug the ladder back to the barn and put away the tools. I managed to be sittin' on the front steps when the Model A chugged to a stop in front of the house.

Ma and Pa got out and started up the path toward me. They started to walk slower and began turnin' their heads left and right like they were lookin' for somethin'. I started whistlin' to show I didn't have a care.

They stopped right in front of me and Ma gave me that look.

"What? I'm not doin' anything," I said, like butter wouldn't melt in my mouth.

"What? You tell me what," Ma said. Now, she stood with her fists on her hips and her mouth gettin' tight. Pa kind of turned to one side and I could see he was tryin' to keep from smilin'.

I let out my breath kind of slow and hung my head. I was thinkin' fast and furious now. Should I go ahead and tell her about the clothesline? After all, it was fixed good as new. Or, maybe I should just keep quiet and let Ma have her suspicions.

Dorothy came to the door suckin' on a jawbreaker so big her mouth was full. Still, she managed to open it just a little bit more. "Eddie shot down the clothesline, Ma."

I looked at Sister with what I hoped was a promise she was goin' get it, but good.

Pa started laughin' out loud at this point. I don't think he ever took anything too serious as long as there weren't no blood involved.

Ma grabbed me by the collar and we took the long, slow walk out to the woodshed. She glanced over at the clothesline as we went by and saw I'd fixed it up. I hoped it would let her hand go a bit easy. I was right and I only got three good switches.

Sister will keep one eye open tonight, but I think I'll just wait to get back at her when she least expects it.

The Luck Brothers

While nobody lived close enough so you could talk over the fence, there were neighbors. Some of them were just a bit stranger than the others.

FRED AND FRANK Luck lived up the road about six miles. We didn't have much to do with them, but one time we, meanin' Pa and me, had to go visiting. They was an odd pair, bein' identical twins who purely hated each other. Their ma died  when she birthed them and their pa pretty much let them go wild. A few of the womenfolk hereabouts helped out when they were just babies, but once they got to ten or so, they pretty much did what they pleased.

After the boys grew up, their pa died and they inherited the farm equal between them. Fred wanted to sell the farm, take his share, and move to Houston. Frank wanted to keep the farm, so he didn't allow it to be sold. That was the start of their feudin' and they'd been at each other ever since.

My Aunt Lyddie, Pa's sister, had a daughter Eva, who started actin' wild when she was seventeen or thereabouts. Well, that's what Aunt Lyddie said anyway. Eva finished up with school and took to hangin' round at the Luck's place.

One day, Aunt Lyddie come up the road in her wagon drawn up by her old horse Ned. She never did get the hang of startin' up her Model T, though she bought one first thing they come to Lubbock. Pa and me went up and helped her down from the wagon.

"Louis," she says to Pa, "you gotta hep me get Eva way from the Luck boys. She ain't been home for the last week and I'm afeared she's goin' to . . ." She looks down at me and says, "well, you know."

Pa replied, "Whatever's goin' to happen probably already did, Lyddie. Not much we can do about it now."

"Still, I don't want her up with the Lucks. Those boys go crazy sometimes and she might get hurt if'n she comes between 'em."

"Well, now, don't fret none, Lyddie. Me and the boy here will drive on up there and see what we can do."

This seemed to satisfy Lyddie, who proceeded to go up to the house to visit awhile with Ma.

Pa turned to me and says, "Wanna go for a drive, Eddie?"

"Sure, Pa." It was fine with me as I'd been cleanin' out the chicken yard and anything'd be better than that chore.

Pa and I pushed the Model A out of the barn and cranked her up. We jumped in and proceeded up the road to the Luck's farm.

It didn't take but a half hour to drive the six miles. When we were gettin' close, we heard the sound of a shotgun firin' off. As we pulled off onto the road leadin' up to the Luck's house, we heard shoutin' as well.

Pa looked at me and says, "Be sure to watch close and be ready to duck down behind the truck."

It made me a little nervous. It was well known Fred and Frank would go at each other just about anyplace they happened to be. Once, they both spent a night in jail when they got into a fist fight at the General Store. The Sheriff didn't much care which one started it, so he just let them both spend the night in the pokey. He let 'em out early enough to go take care of the livestock and didn't do anything else.

Now, they pretty much kept their fightin' at home. Most often they'd just flail at each other for awhile and then one or t'other would go off in a huff. Hearin' gunfire made me think the feud was only gettin' worse.

When we get up to the farmyard, we saw Frank, or maybe it was Fred, standin' by the corral kind of hid behind a post and he was firin' off shotgun blasts toward the granary. We could see the wood splinter as he fired. I glimpsed the other one, most likely Fred, around the side of the building.

"Frank, you cut that out!" Pa shouted.

"I ain't Frank, Mr. Perkins," the shotgun holder answered back.

"Well, then, Fred, you cut that out."

"But, Mr. Perkins, that no-good brother o' mine called me a dirty lowdown skunk. I can't rightly take it without answerin'!"

Pa motioned to me to stand behind the truck bed and I went round as quick as I could. Pa started walkin' slow toward Fred movin' his hands in a placatin' way.

"Well, I'm sure you two can work it out if'n you'll just put the gun away, Fred."

Then, Pa calls out louder. "Frank, come on out."

"No sirree! I ain't crazy, Mr. Perkins. That idiot will just shoot me if'n I come out," Frank yelled, peekin' round the corner of the granary.

While the talkin' was goin' on, Pa kept gettin' closer to Fred until he was an arm's reach away. He grabbed the double barrel of the shotgun and snatched it away and tossed the gun behind him about ten feet.

"All right, Frank, you can come out now. Fred doesn't have the shotgun anymore."

Frank come out slow from behind the buildin' lookin' hard to make sure what Pa said was the truth. When he seen Fred didn't have the gun, he walked on over. He gets up a couple of feet away and he lunged out at Fred and grabbed him round the neck.

The brothers fell down on the ground and started wrestlin' and screamin' some pretty bad words.

"You low-down weasel!" Bam! Frank smacked Fred right in the eye.

"You yellow-bellied hornswoggler!" Whap! Fred hit him

right back.

Pa stood there a bit with his hands on his hips. He looked to be ponderin' whether or not to separate them. Finally, he bent down and grabbed both the Lucks by their collars and hauled them right up on their feet. My jaw dropped as I didn't think Pa had it in him. He held 'em both at arms length until they quit strugglin', then he let them go.

Frank feints to the right like he's tryin' to get round Pa, but it didn't do him no good. Pa just stuck out his arm straight and slammed ol' Frank right in the chest. I thought it was Frank, anyways. With both of them wearin' coveralls, there's not much to tell the difference between 'em.

Finally, they settled down some when they saw Pa wouldn't let 'em go at it again.

"Now, you boys can start up again when we're gone, but while I'm here you'll be actin' the straight and narrow."

The two of them nodded with their heads downcast some. I think Pa'd taken the fight out of 'em for now.

Then, Pa says, "We only come up here to fetch Eva. Where is she?"

Frank, or Fred, jerked his thumb over his shoulder at the house. I looked over and saw Eva at the doorway. Pa walked up to her and takes her by the arm.

"You all better get back home, Eva. Your ma's worried about you."

She glanced over at the Luck boys, but saw they weren't

going to stop her from leavin', so she just sighed and walked over to the truck and got in. The Luck boys just stood there like they were waitin' for us to leave.

I jumped into the truck bed and Pa started it up. As we was headin' toward the road, I was lookin' back and saw one of the Lucks shove the other on the shoulder, then they were down on the ground again walin' away on each other. I was sure glad I didn't have a twin brother if'n this is how they behaved.

We bounced back down the road to our place, where Aunt Lyddie was still waitin' with Ma. They came out of the house when they saw us drive up. Aunt Lyddie headed straight over to the truck, opened the door, and drug Eva out. There was fire in her eyes, and I almost felt sorry for Eva.

Pa pointed to the chicken yard. I heaved a big sigh. The excitement was over and there was still chores to be done.

Didn't make any difference anyhow, as she went back up to the Luck's place the next day. She ended up marrying one of 'em. Must have been Fred 'cause they moved to Houston.

Ma's Story

Mothers have their own joys and sorrows. Too often they keep their feelings to themselves and even their own families don't know.

WHEN I WAS a boy, my Ma was a woman of few words, which surprised quite a few folks. The town ladies came out to visit on occasion and she'd go to town to return the favor, but mostly she listened. That did set her apart from the gossipers and them that just liked to talk to hear themselves.

Ma married Pa when she was only eighteen years old. Pa was married before and got divorced, which was pretty unusual at the time. Flossie, Pa's first wife, had a son name of Harley, but we didn't ever see them. So, Pa was somewhat older than Ma and I think she was quiet out of respect for her elders.

I didn't really notice this when I was a kid, but only started thinking about it after she died. I wanted to remember everything I could, so that's why I wrote down some of the stories. This here's Ma's story as I think she would have told it herself.

§ § §

When I first met Louis, I was surprised, but pleased, an older man would be interested in me. I didn't even know he was my cousin until the day we met. My mother told me we were related on her side of the family, but I didn't ever figure out how it was. Maybe we weren't actual cousins, but somehow we shared family a ways back.

Louis was fifteen years my senior. He'd been married, had a child, and gone to war. All this set him apart from the boys my own age. He was a gentle man and a gentleman, as I liked to describe him. He was always 'please' and 'thank you,' and 'after you miss.' It seemed like he took to me pretty quick, 'cause he wasn't a shy man, neither.

We got married in Iowa, but moved off to Oklahoma when we were still newlyweds. Louis tried running a general store, but that made him restless, I think. When Edward, our first son, was born, we packed up and moved south to Hereford, Texas. Louis saved up enough for us to lease a farm. It was a nice place with six hundred forty acres we kept in wheat, sorghum, and corn. We had a good business raising pigs.

Of course, we owned horses. I swear, Louis couldn't live without a horse or two around. He'd been a horse doctor when he was in the World War in France. We also kept a few breeding jackasses, and charged out their services to the other farmers hereabouts. I do recall the problems with Bucephalus the jackass, or Beau as we called him. It makes me laugh when I think of the time when he nearly choked himself to death. Not that it would be funny if'n he'd choked, mind you, only it was funny the look on little Eddie's face when he come runnin' licketysplit into the house demanding I give him a butcher knife. I had to stop him and settle him down to find out Beau was needin' rescue.

Not long after that incident, Dorothy was born. Oh, she was the apple of her father's eye, no doubt about it. She was such a pretty little girl and followed Edward around like a pup. They went ever'where together.

One summer, we sent the two of them down south to visit the Porter family, cousins of mine. They sure did have an adventure then. They'd spent a good part of the summer collectin' cow bones and sellin' them to make a little money. When they were out one day, they'd rode clear over into New Mexico and met up with a young man there. He'd showed them some mammoth bones, fossils he called them, he'd found in Blackwater Draw.

When Eddie and Sister were eight and four, if I recall, we had Mary Ada. She was sickly born and never did get much better. It broke me when she died of typhoid. She just wasn't strong enough to fight it off. I was broken up more'n I thought by her dyin'. It wasn't 'til years later I understood how I'd kind of, well, shut down. I'm ashamed I quit carin' much about anything.

Mrs. Walters next door would have those afternoon teas,

with fine china and silver and little sandwiches with the crusts cut off. After some urging by Louis, I went to one wearin' my blue-checked Sunday dress and white gloves with the little pearls on them. I listened to the ladies talk about children and recipes and laundry soap and such, but my heart wasn't in it. My heart wasn't in my other children either. I'm even sorrier to admit that.

I did come out of it some when James and John were born less'n two years apart. With two little boys to take care of, I didn't have any choice but to come around. I guess I'd just mourned long enough.

Those years between Mary Ada dyin' and James being born, I let Edward and Dorothy go their own way. I was fortunate Eddie had a good head on his shoulders and that he looked after Sister.

My, but those two went all over the place by themselves. They rode their horses to school every day. One time Sister nearly got killed when they crossed a rain-swelled creek on the way to school. I was none too happy with Edward about that. That was one time he didn't show good sense. He'll tell you all about it, so I don't need to go into details here.

When Edward grew up and left home, we sure did miss him. He was in the army and met a nice girl named Iva he wanted to marry, and he did just that. He wrote us letters tellin' about the Pacific Northwest, sayin' it was a beautiful place and he'd taken an interest loggin'.

By this time, Louis was wearin' down some, so we thought

it a good time to quit the oil business and move to Oregon. We ended up livin' there for many years.

I took to the nursing profession and got my degree. I worked at a clinic for many years. When I retired, I moved around from child to child, but spent most of my time with Dorothy as she needed me the most. I lived in Texas again for awhile after Louis died. My sister Alma and her children lived in Dallas and were very good to me when I stayed down there. Her family got rich off the oil wells. Alma's husband, John, got hurt bad workin' the oil rigs and he lived out most his life in the hospital. He'd got himself hit in the head with a pipe and he wasn't ever right after that. Alma's boys took over the business and made good.

At the end, though, I moved down to Florida to stay with Dorothy and her husband, Tex. Once in awhile I went back up to Oregon to visit the family who stayed there. That was just about everyone else as Edward, John, and Jim all stayed put once they got up that way. But, Dorothy was my only daughter. Maybe it would have been different if Mary Ada had lived. That's the whole story of my life.

§ § §

Ma's a modest woman and doesn't say all the things she done. Raisin' four kids out in West Texas on a farm was hard work, especially for a woman, and more especially when the Great Depression made life so hard. I'll always think of her as a brave woman and I'll always love her for bein' my Ma.

Cage McNatt's Prize Sow

Even small towns can come up with odd characters. Cage McNatt had to be one of the oddest.

I'VE HEARD OF men gettin' all fired up about their horses. I'd even heard of a man who had a steer he took with him duck huntin'. But, I still can't understand how Cage McNatt was so taken with a pig. After all, a pig generally ends up bein' ham and pork chops, but Cage McNatt was mighty fond of his sow. He even named her, which is unusual right there. He called her Petunia, which I thought was a darned silly name for anything, even a pig.

I suppose there was some sense as to why he was so taken with her. He did win every year at the county fair. She was a beauty, no doubt about that. I just thought Mr. McNatt went a little far, especially the time Fred Luck entered his sow, too.

As was usual durin' the Deaf Smith County Fair, my Pa's friend Dad Boles showed up to sell bobcat skins and to pit his tame bear Sophie against the local dogs. This is also when the carnival comes to town, so it was just about the high point of my year.

Now, when I said Dad Boles bear was put up against the dogs, it weren't done mean-like. It weren't no bear baitin'. He'd just tie up Sophie to a post and the dogs were let loose to come at her. She'd usually just give 'em a good slap on the muzzle and they'd give up real quick.

But, this story is about Cage McNatt's pig. Both the McNatt and the Luck pigs were entered in the fair and it was pretty clear to everybody these were the only contenders for the blue ribbon. The rest of the sows were fine, but didn't come up to these two. They weighed close to the same. I heard three hundred fifty pounds or thereabouts. Petunia was all black and the Luck sow, which was named Whitey, was white. I thought Petunia looked smaller, but I suppose that might've been her color.

Pa let me camp with Dad Boles for a day or two as it was fifteen miles from our farm to Hereford and I liked to go to the fair on more than one day. Dad Boles didn't seem to mind my company. He told me a few stories about his trapping business and about his time in France with Pa during the World War.

Each evening, when the fair was over, Dad would untie Sophie from her post and let her sit closer to the fire. One night, after things calmed down, Dad Boles and I were sittin' by the fire with Sophie right next to us. Dad Boles was in the middle of a story about trappin' when we heard something crashin' around inside the fairgrounds. Dad decided to go see what was goin' on and I followed along since he didn't say to stay put. We went into the fairgrounds to see what was up. The moon was full so we could see well enough.

A man was goin' toward the fairgrounds' front gate and it looked like he was pullin' a big dog along behind him. When I heard the squeal, though, I realized it wasn't a dog, but a pig. I could also see the pig was white, so I knew right off it was the Luck's sow. The trouble was that the man was Cage McNatt and not one of the Luck brothers.

Well, you might already have guessed what was goin' on. Cage McNatt was stealin' Whitey, or at least he was tryin' to. The problem was Whitey was bigger than Mr. McNatt and she wasn't of a mind to go along quiet. She was doin' her best to pull away from the rope. She was shakin' her head back and forth and kept up squealin' the whole time. That was about the unhappiest pig I ever saw.

Then, she spotted the open gate. She quit squealin', snorted a couple of times, and all of a sudden she was doin' the pullin' and Cage McNatt was runnin' behind her tryin' to keep up. She was makin' a beeline for the gate where we just happened to be standin'. I figured we'd better just step out of the way. Bein' run down by three hundred fifty pounds of hog flesh was not an idea I cottoned to.

What I didn't realize, and Whitey didn't either, was Sophie followed us through the gate. She, meanin' Whitey, got about twenty feet from us when she looked up and saw a bear standin' in the way of her freedom. She stopped short and Cage McNatt ran right by her as he had such a head of steam goin'. When he reached the end of the rope, it came right out of his hand. I could see her sittin' down on her haunches and starin' at Sophie like she was wonderin' exactly what it was she was seein'. All she knew is it was a big, hairy critter and probably smelled pretty bad, too.

The sow made up her mind. She whipped around like she was a cuttin' horse and headed in the opposite direction. I think Sophie was gettin' curious about this activity, so she went along after the pig. We took out runnin' as well. Dad Boles didn't want to risk Sophie harmin' any livestock, so he was in a big hurry to catch up with her.

I was runnin' right behind Dad Boles and I heard Cage McNatt's footsteps right behind me.

The sow headed straight for the Ferris Wheel. I could see one of the cars was at the bottom and it was open. I think you've guessed what came next. The pig jumped up into the car and it shuddered like it was hit by a tornado. The gate on the car slammed shut and the pig was jumpin' around and the car was rockin' somethin' furious.

Sophie followed on up the ramp to get to the pig. I don't think she meant any harm, but was just curious. Sophie went to one side of the ramp then to the other lookin' for an opening to the car. As she stepped to the right, she pushed up against the lever that ran the wheel. The Ferris Wheel started up and the pig was bein' hoisted up along with it. That seemed to baffle Sophie, so she just stepped off the ramp and walked calm as you please back to Dad Boles.

All three of us stood and watched the car go up with the pig in it squealin' like she was bein' introduced to the slaughterhouse.

Dad came to his senses first and ran up the ramp. He hit the lever and the wheel stopped with the pig's car about halfway up. Now, he wasn't sure what to do as it seemed the only way to get the pig back down would be to start the wheel back up. I think he felt sorry for the pig as it was cryin' like a baby and was clearly real scared to be up so high.

By this time, the carnival folks had come out of their trailers to see what was goin' on. The head man ran over to the wheel and started it back up again. He'd already seen the only way to get the pig down was to run her clear round the circle 'til the car come to earth again. Unlike Dad Boles, he didn't mind givin' the pig the rest of the ride.

The sow made the trip safe enough. When the car reached the bottom, the carnival man opened the gate and she took off like a streak of lightnin'. Dad Boles started laughin' so hard he could hardly stand up. In between his guffawin', Dad Boles couldn't help but say, "Well, I never figured I'd ever really see a pig fly."

Well, the end of the story was the judges made Cage McNatt take Petunia out of the competition. The Luck brother's sow, Whitey, won the blue ribbon and a few lesser sows took the other ribbons. It did make for one of the most interestin' fairs and every year after somebody always told the story of the time Cage McNatt made a pig fly.

Crossin' the Creek

Kids went to school, but they didn't exactly catch the school bus outside the house. Getting to school could be an adventure.

IT'D BEEN RAINING forty days and forty nights is what Ma said, but I only counted up eleven days myself. She did tend to put things in Bible verses, so I won't say she was lyin', just exaggeratin' for effect.

Still, me and my sister, Dorothy, who we called Sister, had to go to school, whether the creek was high or dry. We'd spent Saturday and Sunday hopin' the rain would at least slow down some, but it didn't look like it was going to. On Monday, we put on our rain slickers and ran to the barn quick as we could to saddle the horses. Pa cut out oiled canvas to cover the saddles and most of the horse as well.

Brownie and Peaches saw us comin' and they crowded back in the barn behind the cows tryin' to pretend they wasn't there. We dragged 'em out by the halter since they were none too fond of goin' out in the rain. Couldn't say I blamed 'em, as I wasn't too fond of it myself.

Our school was more'n six miles away, so we got an early start every mornin', along about five, so we could get there by seven. Usually, Sister and me would just let loose on the reins and let the horses go at their own pace. Brownie and Peaches knew the way, as they went to school just as often as we did. But, on days with the rain sheetin' down, none of us was in a hurry to leave the barn. It took some effort, particularly with Peaches as she tended to hate gettin' wet more than Brownie.

Off we went down the road, usually dusty, was now fetlock deep in mud. We'd have to go slow or the horses would slipslide off the road and into the ditch.

We had to cross a creek along the way. This creek was only a few inches deep most of the time and only five feet across, but after this rain, the water reached near to Peaches' belly. She was one unhappy pony, I can tell you that.

We got to the creek and saw the brown water rushin' along. It was up on the banks and a good fifteen feet across. I'd never seen it this high and I was gettin' worried some.

We was already soakin' wet, but it didn't matter to Peaches. She took one look and you could almost hear her say, "I'm not goin' across that!" She set her feet and didn't take another step.

The plan was to tie a rope onto her bridle with the other end round my saddlehorn, so I could lead her across. But, she was havin' none of it. She set back on her haunches just like a dog sittin' down. It was actually pretty funny-lookin', but I didn't say so as Sister was gettin' a mite agitated.

"We can just leave Peaches over at the Tate's and we can double up on Brownie," I suggested.

"No, I want her to do what she's supposed to do," Sister grumbled. Even with her squeaky little girl's voice, she made it clear she wouldn't brook no nonsense from Peaches.

"It's up to you, Sister. I'll pull her ahead, but you gotta show her who's boss."

"Don't you worry, Eddie. I don't like to do it, but I'll give her a whup to let her know I mean business." Sister seemed determined to not let Peaches get away with anything, so I just shrugged and started on across the creek.

Brownie stopped when he felt the tug of the rope with Peaches at the other end, not movin'. Sister took up the long end of the reins and gave Peaches a swat on the haunch. That startled her enough to get her up on all fours, then I nudged Brownie with my heels and he started to draggin' Peaches behind him. He just wanted to get across the creek, so was not of a mind to let Peaches slow him down.

Peaches sat back down again and no amount of swattin' got her up. I brought Brownie back to her side of the creek. I sussed what was goin' on and thought puttin' the rope around her neck would encourage her to move. Looking back, I don't figure it was such a good idea.

I got the rope tied around her neck and made sure it wasn't a slipknot, then wound it tight around the saddlehorn. After all, I didn't want to strangle her, just get her movin'.

"Do you want to get on Brownie with me while we cross?" I was a little concerned about what Peaches would do, but I knew Brownie was steady.

"Nope. If I do that, then Peaches won't move for nothin'. I've got stay on to make her go," Sister said. She was gettin' as stubborn as Peaches by now. I shrugged and started Brownie up again. He was still willin', but anxious to get across as quick as he could.

About half-way across, I could see the water was higher than I thought as it was brushin' up on Brownie's belly. This was worrisome, as Peaches was smaller than Brownie and she'd be in water up to her shoulder.

Finally, though, she started across. If a horse can have an expression on its face, I'd say Peaches looked about as mad as could be. Her ears were laid back and she was shakin' her head back and forth tryin' to lose the rope. It did her no good and we just kept on goin'.

When the water reached Peaches' belly, the oil cloth started to billow out on the water like a big, shiny square dance skirt. I could tell she was gettin' scared. Her eyes were rollin' in her head and her nostrils were puffin' in and out. She kept shakin' her head like she was sayin' no.

"Now, Peaches, just a few more feet and we'll be up the other side. The worst's over. C'mon, girl, you can do it," Sister leaned forward and encouraged Peaches as best she could. I could tell Sister was a little worried about how deep the water was, too.

Now, the water was comin' up over Peaches' shoulder and it was clear she was one scared pony. Sister kept pattin' and whisperin' to her, but Peaches couldn't take no more.

She reared back and hit the top of her head right in Sister's face. Then, quick as can be, Peaches lunged forward and jumped right by me and Brownie. She was movin' so fast, she almost pulled the saddle right off Brownie. All I could think of was if Brownie fell, he would drag Peaches and Sister right after him. All at the same time, I was tryin' to help Brownie keep his feet under him, keep' an eye on Sister, and workin' on gettin' the darned rope off the saddlehorn.

I could see Sister was swayin' on the saddle and it scared me awful. She almost fell, then grabbed to the saddlehorn and pulled herself back on. Brownie got his feet under him and followed Peaches up on the bank.

We got to the other side and Peaches stopped. She stood with her head down and her legs shakin'. I looked at Sister's face and saw blood, but it looked like it was just a bloody nose.

We all stood still for awhile. I got down and took the rope off Peaches. I was wonderin' whether we could get her movin' again. Soon as I was up in the saddle, though, Peaches picked her head back up and started off toward school. Sister managed to haul out her handkerchief from under her slicker and was holdin' it against her nose. I figured we could fix her up when we got to school.

"Sister, you all right?" I was worried whether she'd been knocked silly, but she nodded her head.

"I'm fine," she said loud enough as she looked right at the pony's ears. I knew she was tryin' to convince Peaches everything was all right. Peaches' ears twitched back, so I guessed she was listenin'. When we got to school, the rain eased up and some sun started shinin' through the clouds.

Our teacher took Sister in-hand and cleaned her up whilst I put Brownie and Peaches in the barn. It burned my hide there was only five of us what showed up. Nobody else had the bad sense to go out on a day like this.

I hoped the creek would go down before we headed back for home. I wouldn't care to repeat the experience.

The Thief

The Great Depression was beginning to seep into the lives of the people in West Texas. Insulated to some extent, they began to see the repercussions of the droughts by the people who came south from Oklahoma for relief from the dust storms.

IT ALWAYS MEANS a good time when Pa lets me go with him in the truck. I liked the truck a lot and sometimes he'd let me drive a ways, too. This time, Pa planned on goin' further than Hereford. We were goin' to go to Amarillo, the trip some fifty miles. It would take us most of one day to get there and do what we needed to do, so we'd have to camp overnight somewhere along the way.

Amarillo was pretty big as cities go up here in the panhandle. The only other big town was Lubbock, which was south of us and about a hundred miles away.

We was to find out the droughts were just beginning in 1932 in Oklahoma, but the people was already sufferin' for it. For one thing, a lot of folks from Oklahoma began to move down here to Texas 'cause it wasn't as bad. It was so dry up north all the good soil just started blowin' away ever' time the wind came up.

The worst was the black blizzards, which come up so sudden nobody could do anything about it. The storm would rise up like a long wall of muddy water maybe seven or eight thousand feet high and come in a big wave across the prairie.

It was worse'n the tornadoes which sometimes came along right after. Pa said the dust would cover everything and even strangle the livestock right out in the field. When there was no water and only dust as far as the eye could see, farmers were forced to pack up what they could and head west and sometimes south to Texas.

Those who came south didn't choose very well, 'cause the droughts were beginnin' to come down our way, too. The people came for the oil wells, but there weren't enough jobs for everyone. Most of 'em went on the dole and just traveled around lookin' for work wherever they could. Pa hired a couple of men last season, but he couldn't keep them on. We had just enough for ourselves he said. It did break his heart to turn them away, but there wasn't nothin' he could do about it.

We was lucky so far, but Pa thought things would get worse before they got better. Still, we put in good crops, the pig business was doin' fine, and Pa did a lot of veterinary work as he had learned the skill from the army.

So, we traveled to Amarillo to do some shoppin'. Ma sent orders to get a new iron skillet, so we went to the Woolworths Five and Dime store for that. Pa picked up some heavy gloves and some other odds and ends. Then, we stopped at the fountain for an ice cream sundae. I sat at the counter and watched while the soda jerk dished out two whole scoops of vanilla, a whole ladle of chocolate sauce, and a mess of whipped cream. He even topped it with a cherry. It was almost too pretty to eat, but I ate it anyway. That was somethin' we didn't get very often.

We packed up what we'd bought in the truck and spent some time to look around before headin' back home. It was late in the day, so we'd be stoppin' somewhere along the road overnight. In the meantime, we took a little tour of the big city and got supper from a man sellin' hotdogs right on the street. I was too stuffed to eat any more, so we got in the truck and headed back to home.

We drove out of town and stopped in an oak grove as the sun was goin' down. It was clear people stayed here often, 'cause there were stone circles where campfires go. Pa built a little fire. Ma'd packed some cornbread for us, but we were still too full to eat it. We'd brought along blankets and we spent the night comfortable enough under the big oak trees. Late in the night, I woke up to hear some more folks comin' in the grove. They was quiet enough, and I soon went back to sleep.

Just before dawn, though, I got woke up again. I saw somebody creepin' around by the truck. I looked to Pa, but he was snorin' away. I thought maybe the person was just goin' by, but then I could see they was openin' the truck door real slow. Now, I knew he were lookin' to steal something. I didn't think there was anything of value in the truck 'cept Ma's skillet, but it's the principle as Pa says.

I jumped up and ran over to the truck. The thief was on the far side and didn't see me yet. I stopped and snuck around the front of the truck quiet as I could. When I got closer, I could see the thief was rummagin' through the truck lookin' for whatever he could steal. The door was open between him and me, so I just jumped forward real fast and slammed the truck door right on him.

A scream so loud they could hear it back in town came out of him. I was taken aback some as it was real high and sounded a whole lot like my sister when she was yellin' about somethin' I did.

I was holdin' the door shut on him and he was strugglin' to get out from the trap. I leaned up against the door and pushed in with my heels hard as I could.

I could see Pa jump up from his bedding and come runnin' over. He went round the back of the truck, so he could grab the thief. He nodded his head once he got hold of his arm and I let go of the door. Pa pulled him out and threw him right on the ground.

Everybody in the camp got woke up by the commotion and come runnin' over to see what was happenin'. One of them was a big man, wearin' the overalls farmers always wore. He walked straight up to the thief layin' on the ground and pulled him up by his collar.

When he did that, we could see the thief was a girl. She was dressed in pants, a coat three sizes too big for her and a hat pulled down over her ears. I could see she was about my age and I started feelin' sorry I'd smashed her with the door.

The man seemed to be her father. He started a'shakin' her and he was yellin' pretty loud, too. She started cryin' and I felt ten times worse. If'n I knowed she was a girl, I wouldn't have been so rough on her. Still, she was thievin' and that was wrong.

Her pa was still shakin' her and yellin' in her face. Those words shouldn't ought to be said to anybody, least of all his own daughter. I was gettin' summat distressed as I ain't ever heard anybody that mad at their own kin.

Pa stepped forward and held his hand against the man's chest, not like he was pushin' but just like he'd do with a horse to settle it down.

"Take it easy. No harm done here," Pa said quiet-like.

"She's a damned thief," the man yelled, then he slapped her hard across the face.

Pa hauled back his fist and shot it right into the man's jaw. It dropped him like a rock and he fell on his back. The girl took the opportunity to skedaddle over to her ma.

"Now, sir, that is no way to treat a girl and it is no way for you to speak in front of my son here."

I thought the man would yell at Pa or he'd get up and try to fight him. But he didn't. Instead, he started to cry and he held his face in his hands and started sobbin'. I was purely shocked at this turn of events. Pa let him go on for a short time, then he reached his hand down to help the man up.

"I'm sorry, I'm sorry," the man gasped for breath.

"It's all right. You just shouldn't be treatin' your girl like that. It ain't proper."

As the sun was now comin' up, everyone started to go back to their own camps to start up their fires again. The man walked slowly over to his own camp. I was glad to see him put his arm around the girl's shoulders. She flinched back some, but he spoke to her quiet then she wrapped her arms around him. They stood there holdin' on to each other, like family should.

As we boiled up some coffee and got the cornbread out for breakfast, Pa tol' me these folks had lost everything to the dust.

"Sometimes, you can't blame a person if they go too far, if they'd already been pushed too far," he said. He shook his head and I saw he was sad. I was sad, too.

We packed up our gear. Pa took the rest of the cornbread and went over to the family's campsite. He handed the package to the girl's mother, then talked to the man for a few minutes. I saw them shake hands and Pa came back and tol' me to get in the truck.

Once we were headed down the road, Pa said, "We'll be seein' those folks in a couple of days."

"Why, Pa? Are they comin' to visit us?"

"I'm hirin' John, that's his name, on for a few days."

"But, Pa, you said we just had enough for us to get by. You quit hirin' people on last season."

"I know, I know," he said and didn't speak for awhile.

Then, he said, "We just have enough to get by, that's true. But, if folks don't have enough to even live, then we just have to make do with a bit less."

"Yessir, Pa. I can see how's that's the right thing to do."

We drove on home mostly quiet the rest of the way. When we got home and Pa took Ma aside to tell her we'd be havin' company, she shook her head, but not like she was sayin' no. She tol' me to get out to the chicken coop and see if those hens didn't lay a few more eggs. She had some bakin' to do.

Chance Encounter

All kids eventually grow up, but in that in-between time interesting things can happen. When Eddie moved to East Texas and began High School, he joined the football team. The team was good enough to go to the State Championship. Along the way, he meets a woman who turns his head around.

LIFE WAS TOUGH in the 30s, but people didn't complain, they just tried to get along as best they could. When I was gettin' in my teen years, times were tough enough that Pa decided we'd move the family to East Texas. The reason for this is in one word: oil. My uncle Alex started up in the oil business and he'd invited Pa to come help out. This was fine with Ma, as Uncle Alex married her sister Alma.

So we packed up the furnishings and moved out of the farmhouse. I'd only just found out Pa didn't own the farm we'd worked near Hereford, but was just a tenant. He'd never said and I'd never asked, but that fact gave me some understandin' of why things were the way they were. Since we didn't own our land, it left us high and dry when the droughts moved down our way. I believe the owner decided to sell the land to one of the ranches, and we didn't have a place to live anymore.

When I got to high school, I didn't know anybody, but I found out I was good at sports. That helped me fit into my new school. I played football, basketball, and bein' a fast runner, I also took to the track events. Football was my favorite, mostly 'cause folks liked to watch the football games more'n the others.

Our team, the Salem Wildcatters, did pretty well in 1937 and we ended up winnin' the district championship. It was a big deal for the school to win, so us on the team were feelin' pretty proud of ourselves when we were told we'd be goin' to Dallas for the State Championship.

Now, we didn't figure to win, because just about the entire junior and senior classes were on the team. I was a junior that year. That meant the coach didn't have much to pick and choose from. But, we got lucky and beat out the rest of the schools within a hundred miles or so.

The school hired a bus to take us to Dallas and our mothers packed us all big lunches to take along. We figured to take the bus up to Highway 20 and then head west to Dallas. We were pretty excited and did a lot of jokin' around and even some singin' on the bus. Sister, that bein' what we called my sister Dorothy, was goin' to come up the next day with the band and they'd get to play durin' our game. We were playin' against a Dallas team, so we expected we'd play just the one time.

We'd got on to Highway 20 and traveled a piece when the coach said to take a stop for lunch and to allow us to use the facilities. That meant we stopped at a gas station with a little diner sittin' next to it. Some of the boys were well off and decided they'd eat lunch at the diner. I had the lunch Ma packed, but went to the diner with the other guys to get myself a Coke.

It was crowded in the diner as it only held around twenty people, if that. In one booth at the far end of the diner there sat one of the prettiest women I'd ever seen. Her hair was all curled up and she was wearin' lipstick and blue stuff on her eyelids. A fur wrapped around her shoulders, even though it was plenty warm outside. She was sittin' with a man and another woman, but it was hard to see anybody but her in that booth.

I saw some of the other boys stop and whisper to each other while they were lookin' at her. She smiled at us and seemed friendly enough.

I went up to the counter to buy my Coke and saw her lookin' my way. I turned to her and gave her a smile, wantin' to be polite and all. She crooked her finger at me lettin' me know she wanted me to come over. So, I did.

I went over to say howdy and she patted her hand, which had on a glove, on the seat next to her. I sat down, naturally.

She asked me, "what are all you fine-looking boys doing out here?"

"Why, ma'am, we're headin' to Dallas to play in the football championships," I answered respectfully. Up close, I could see she wasn't a really young woman, maybe in her thirties or forties. Still, she was made up nice and smiled so you'd just fall into those blue eyes. I'll have to admit, I was smitten.

She laid her gloved hand on mine and said "You look like you're a runner. I'm guessing you're the quarterback."

I hate to admit I blushed. I answered her, "Actually, I'm a halfback, ma'am."

She actually reached over and squeezed my arm! I was pretty much dumbstruck by that point as I hadn't been this close to a woman like this in my whole life. She sure wasn't like the ladies that lived in town. She wasn't like any lady I'd ever seen. But, at the same time, I got this feeling I knew her from somewhere, I just couldn't place where it was.

"Yes," she said, "nice strong muscles. I can tell you can throw a football really well."

I was beginnin' to get a little dizzy and, I'm truly embarrassed to admit, but I was feelin', well, I'll just say I was feelin'.

She took her hand away from my arm. I think she saw I

was getting embarrassed and all. She talked about this and that for a while. How's the crops been? Has the weather been good? and other such chitchat. Some of the other boys come over and were standin' around the table by that time.

Red, who was my best friend, takes a napkin and hands it to the lady and said, "Please, ma'am, can I have your autograph?" She takes the napkin and signs it for him. The other boys started givin' her pieces of paper to sign, too.

Now, I was truly puzzled. She must be a famous person, but for the life of me, I couldn't place her. I was too embarrassed to ask, since it looked like everybody else knew who she was but me. I figured I shouldn't miss a chance, so I handed her a napkin to sign. When I looked at it, I couldn't make out what it said. Mostly, it just looked like two big circles with some squiggles, so I was none the wiser.

After awhile, she gave me a nudge to get up out of the booth, so I stood up to let her out. She looked around at the boys, since now the entire team was collected at the booth, includin' the coach and the bus driver.

"Well now," she said as she stood up, "I guess you all'd like to see some of the real me." With that, she put her hand on her hip and kind of jutted it out.

With a whole different voice, she said "Come up and see me sometime, boys." Then, she sashayed out of the diner while I stood there with my mouth hangin' open. I felt really stupid when I realized I hadn't recognized Mae West.

Red gave me a nudge and said, "How about that, Ed? Mae West right out here in the middle of nowhere and we got to meet her. Now, we can just lose that old game and it won't bother me at all."

Nope, it wouldn't bother me at all, neither. We did lose the game, but I saw in the Dallas newspaper that Miss Mae West appeared at the Majestic the same time we were in town. Those folks paid good money to see what we got to see for free. I'll never forget the prettiest, and nicest, blond lady I ever did meet.

Made in the USA
Las Vegas, NV
14 May 2022

48877695R00085